500
Patterns

LAURENCE KING

In memory of Anne Townley, without whom
this book may never have been made

Published by Laurence King Publishing Ltd
361–373 City Road
London EC1V 1LR
United Kingdom
Tel: +44 20 7841 6900
E-mail: enquiries@laurenceking.com
www.laurenceking.com

A catalog record for this book is available
from the British Library

ISBN: 978-1-78627-689-6

Commissioning Editor: Sara Goldsmith
Senior Editor: Katherine Pitt
Design: Eleanor Ridsdale

Printed in China

Laurence King Publishing is committed to ethical and sustainable
production. We are proud participants in The Book Chain Project ®
bookchainproject.com

500
Patterns

Jeffrey Mayer | **Todd Conover** | **Lauren Tagliaferro**

Photography by Stephen Sartori

Contents

1970s–80s, USA,
roller-printed
synthetic

1. Half drop repeat
2. Stripe layout
3. Brick pattern repeat
4. Full drop repeat
5. Diamond layout
6. Tossed random layout
7. Ogee layout

The World of Patterns

Patterns surround us. Just look at the natural world, where recurring shapes and lines, neatly organized in their own way, can be found in the symmetry of leaves, plants, and clusters of rose blooms, or the repetition of pebbles on a beach, rings in a tree, and flocks of birds in flight. This natural order has become innate in humans; we see the world in pattern and try to echo its order.

Nowhere is this more obvious than in the creative industry. Since the beginning of time, artists and designers have taken inspiration from their natural environment when designing everything from textiles for fashion and interior design to wall coverings, book covers, and gift wrap. Advertising executives also rely on our, perhaps subconscious, love of orderly repetition and include pattern in commercials, print promotions, and computer graphics. The field of body adornment, such as tattoos and jewelry, also calls on the field of pattern, drawing on both natural and manmade patterns as a rich resource. Pattern is everywhere, when you start to look for it.

The patterns we see around us do not only represent nature, but graphic art, geometric shapes, everyday objects, and even events from popular culture. Take, for example, the small grid pattern on page 124, which was made in 1876 to mark the centennial of the formation of the United States. Essentially, there's nothing that can't be neatly organized into a structured motif.

The art of pattern creation

The majority of the patterns showcased in the book were created between 1840 and 1970, a fruitful time in pattern design. While there are certain big names associated with this period, such as William Morris and Emilio Pucci, most prints were created by anonymous pattern designers, who created great beauty for commerce, rather than as fine art. We have decided to focus on these patterns and motifs, which in many cases have not been seen since their original creation, making them an incredibly useful untapped resource.

In many instances, the staff or freelance artists who created these prints simply started the pattern design process in motion by creating a pleasing motif as a gouache painting. This motif, which may or may not have indicated a preferred method of repeat, was then sent through the standard print production process. A full drop, half drop, or brick repeat would be established, which would then be arranged in a diamond, ogee, tossed pattern, or stripe (see examples opposite). Many hands would be involved in morphing the original artwork into a pattern, not only in developing the repeat, but also by reviewing scale, color, and current trends, to create a pattern suitable for a variety of needs.

A number of techniques were used to create these single and multi-colored patterns on textiles: block printing, in which a carved block of wood is used to apply the dye; perrotine, a mechanized form of block printing; copperplate printing, which is a more refined version of block printing that uses etched copper and allows designers to work in a larger scale; and, finally, roller printing, a copperplated printing technique that employs a cylinder to imprint the pattern as a repeat. To create more precise repeated patterns, some of the more-recent creations were applied to the textiles using flatbed or rotary screen printing, a technique in which dye is forced through a fine mesh that has been treated with a resist and which forms the pattern. The most contemporary patterns shown here were applied using a heat transfer method—picture the classic iron-on transfer. Of course it is now also possible to digitally print pattern onto fabric, but none of the examples included here are recent enough to have employed this technique.

Pattern does not always come in the form of "print," however. It can be woven into the very structure of the cloth using a jacquard loom, to create elaborate brocade designs. Intricate patterns are also formed by applying one material or trim, such as a braid, beads, or embroidery floss, to a base fabric. Further still, designers may layer sheer and opaque textiles, laces, and embroidery together to create a constructed pattern. This last technique may or may not have a repeating motif, but the singular pattern created can still inspire.

A source of inspiration

It is because patterns reflect so many different styles, periods, and ideas that they are such a valuable source of stimulation for creatives, whatever the field. This book, therefore, is intended as a visually invigorating and thought-provoking tool for anyone in search of inspiration. Collecting a personal design library of both images and artifacts is an activity shared by most designers and a natural part of the creative process. Personally collected objects as well as those found in structured collections often provide much-needed inspiration for modern designers, even if the connection to the original image is intangible to the casual observer.

Co-author, jewelry designer, and metalsmith Todd Conover, for instance, often takes visual cues from patterns to create unique pieces. The mood created by a pattern's color or rhythm can even dictate an entire collection of pieces. The midcentury motifs on pages 74, 90, and 106 proved particularly inspiring when Conover was creating a new collection of silver and brass jewelry, and were translated into a brass cuff, a fan-shaped necklace, and the circle within a square brooch.

Upper: Sterling silver necklace by Todd Conover, 2019
Lower: Copper, sterling silver, and brass brooch by Todd Conover, 2019

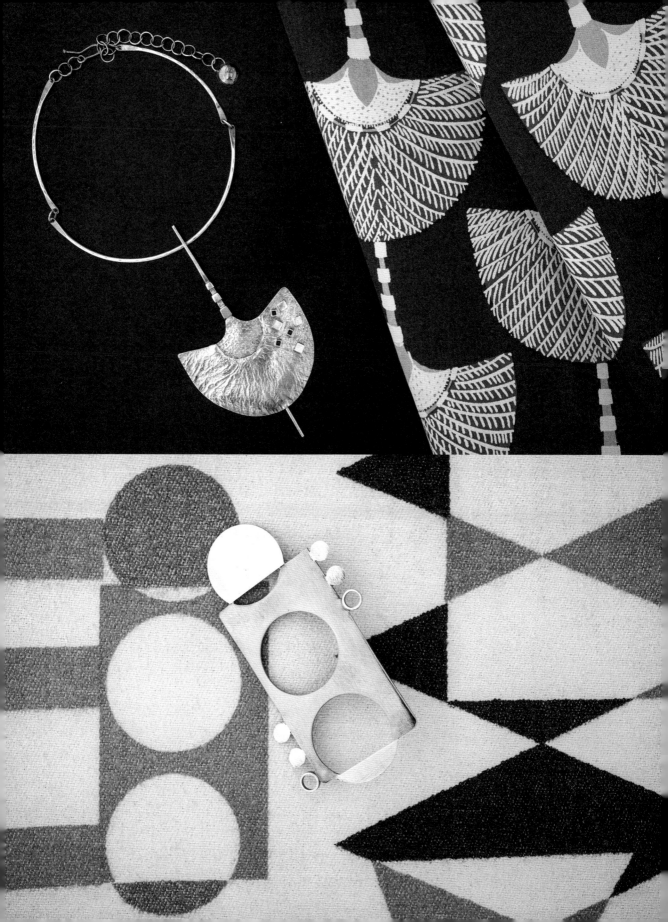

Introducing the patterns

500 Patterns was inspired by the holdings of two magnificent historic clothing and textile repositories in upstate New York, the textile prints of which have never before been showcased or documented.

Like a sleeping beauty, the Rochester Museum & Science Center's historic clothing collection, made up of some 70,000 antique garments, hangs quietly in relative obscurity. This New York State museum began in the early twentieth century as a municipal museum dedicated to the development of a bustling, successful American city. Over the years the focus of the museum has shifted to science and technology, leaving the historic garments safely in private storage for use by researchers. With items starting in the 1830s, the collection's mainstay is a strong holding of American and French couture from the 1890s, continuing through the early 1920s, with highlights by designers such as Charles Worth, Callot Soeurs, and Jeanne Lanvin. The collection terminates in the middle of the twentieth century. The garments in this collection, when viewed in their regimented racks, represent a dazzling kaleidoscope of textile patterns and colors. There are florals of every type, richly colored paisleys, elaborate French brocades, and garment after garment embroidered or embellished with elaborate braid trims, all echoing the economic boom of the Industrial Revolution that was sweeping the globe.

The Sue Ann Genet Costume Collection, located in Syracuse University's College of Visual and Performing Arts, is found in Syracuse, New York. This collection, with its continued support from the family of the late Sue Ann and Leon Genet, is another stronghold of textile pattern. Although its holdings span the later decades of the twentieth century right up to the early twenty-first century, its items from the 1930s through to the 1990s are particularly rich. This extensive collection contains garments made of lavishly patterned fabrics, but it is the rich collection of historic fabric samples, collected from both the United States and Europe, that are particularly exciting.

For maximum visual impact, the patterns in this book have been arranged thematically. The era in which each pattern was created has also been provided, with origins and revivals of motifs placed together for comparison and to allow readers a chance to see these patterns in a different light. All of the patterns featured were photographed from original printed or woven textiles, with the vast majority coming from cut and sewn clothing; these were patterns that people wore and treasured, making them wonderful glimpses into the past.

Finally, a note on scale: to best showcase the patterns and motifs, we have intentionally equalized the scale of each of the patterns, so that all the motifs are on a level playing field. Now the largest mod motif from the 1960s and the smallest Victorian sprig have equal stature, giving each a chance to inspire.

So, whether you are a designer, artist, or tattooist, we hope you will be galvanized creatively by the lush patterns included in this book, and discover myriad ways to incorporate them, however intangibly, into your work.

Brass and carnelian pierced cuff by Todd Conover, 2019

Chapter 1

Floral

Chapter 1

Floral

It is no surprise that floral patterns are so abundant. Flowers are ubiquitous. They delight us with their beauty and evoke powerful sentiments. It seems natural, therefore, that pattern designers would look to the garden for inspiration.

The ways in which flowers are used in pattern design are rich and varied, ranging from the scattered fields of flowers found in small ditsy prints to bold designs developed around very large blooms. Flowers can be randomly scattered in a pattern, as though tossed carelessly into a field, placed precisely for a very orderly appearance, or arranged in stripes. In some instances, flowers are completely abstracted into an impressionistic field of colors and textures that evoke the atmosphere of a garden, rather than a specific bloom.

While almost every type of flower can be found in at least one pattern, there are some that form the building block for most floral arrangements. The rose, for instance, appears to be the queen of the flower bed. Illustrated as a single bloom, in clusters, or mixed into bouquets, the rose transcends time. In Greek mythology, the story of the red rose comes from the tale of Aphrodite. In seeking her lover Adonis's body after his bloody death, she steps on a white rose thorn, puncturing her foot. Her blood stains the white rose a deep red, giving birth to the symbolism of the red rose as a token of endless love and passion.

The poppy also ranks amongst flower royalty. Strong, graphic, and boldly colored,

it is easy to see why this flower is exciting to use visually, but beyond these pleasing optics lies a history steeped in symbolism. Unlike the timeless rose, the poppy is particularly tied to specific eras. Take the unusually lush poppy pattern opposite, which was designed in the early 1920s. The symbolism of these blood-red blooms evokes the solace and remembrance of the poppy fields of Flanders, Belgium, which memorialize the many lost during the First World War. The poppy had another major revival during the youthquake of the late 1960s, when the large and graphic quality of the poppy meshed perfectly with the artistic sentiment of the mod movement, the rule of "flower power," and the longing for a youthful, utopian, free-spirited world.

Not unlike fashion's cyclical interest in the poppy, the sweet, unassuming daisy, so indicative of innocence and purity, came to the fore in the early twentieth century, when these qualities were highly valued in women. Used in profusion for all-over patterned textiles, the always cheerful daisy appears to have been a particular favorite pattern motif during the economically challenged 1930s, when the happy daisy was a small light in the darkness of the tumultuous Depression era. The daisy made a strong comeback again in the 1960s, this time as a rather dramatic pattern motif that fit with the age of flower power perfectly.

c. 1920, France,
roller-printed silk

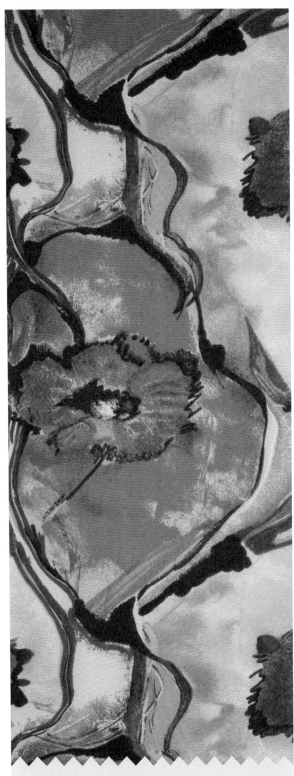

c. 1960, USA, roller-printed cotton

c. 1950, France, roller-printed silk

1930s, USA, roller-printed silk

1930s, USA, roller-printed silk

1920s, USA, roller-printed silk

1940s, USA, roller-printed synthetic

1920s, USA, roller-printed silk

1930s, USA, roller-printed synthetic

1930s, USA, roller-printed synthetic

1920s, USA, roller-printed silk

1930s, USA, roller-printed silk

1960s, USA, roller-printed cotton

1930s, USA, roller-printed silk

1920s, USA, roller-printed silk

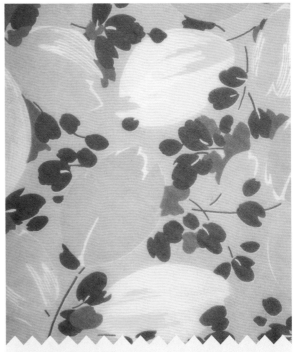

1920s, USA, roller-printed silk

1980s, USA, roller-printed cotton

1970s, USA, heat transfer synthetic

c. 1970, USA, roller-printed cotton

1940s, USA, roller-printed wool

1960s, USA, roller-printed wool

1970s, USA, roller-printed synthetic

1970s, USA, roller-printed synthetic

1970s, USA, roller-printed cotton

1970s, USA, roller-printed synthetic

c. 1967, USA, roller-printed cotton

c. 1967, USA, roller-printed cotton

c. 1925, USA, screen-printed cotton

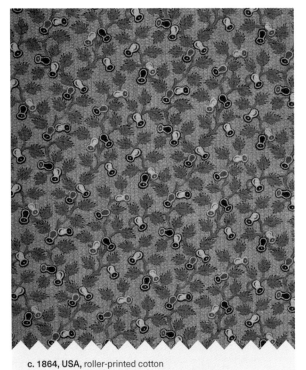

c. 1864, USA, roller-printed cotton

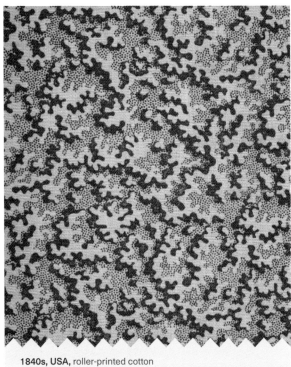

1840s, USA, roller-printed cotton

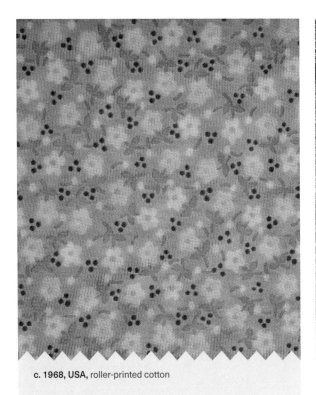

c. 1968, USA, roller-printed cotton

1930s, USA, roller-printed cotton

1970s, USA, roller-printed cotton

1970s, USA, roller-printed cotton

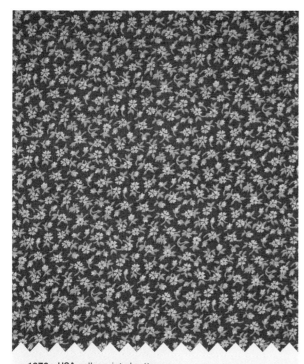

1970s, USA, roller-printed cotton

1970s, USA, roller-printed cotton

1840s, USA, roller-printed cotton

1940s, USA, roller-printed cotton

1920s, USA, roller-printed cotton

1930s, USA, roller-printed synthetic

1930s, USA, roller-printed silk

1940s, USA, roller-printed synthetic

1930s, USA, roller-printed synthetic

1980s, USA, roller-printed cotton

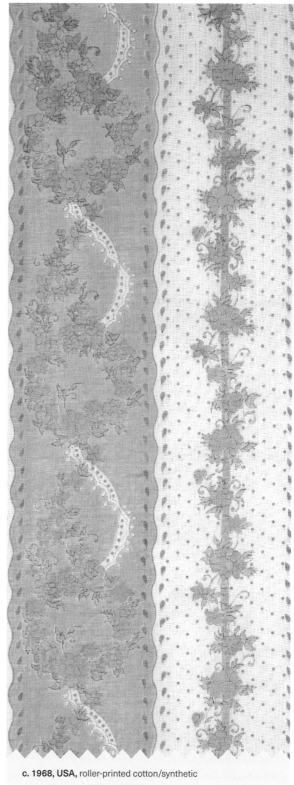

c. 1968, USA, roller-printed cotton/synthetic

1880s, France, roller-printed silk

1880s, USA, roller-printed wool

1890s, USA, roller-printed cotton

1890s, USA, roller-printed silk

1920s, USA, roller-printed wool

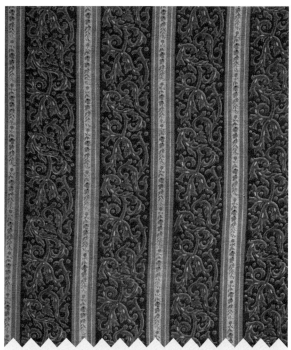

1840s, USA, roller-printed cotton

1890s, USA, roller-printed silk

1890s, USA, roller-printed wool

1920s, USA, roller-printed silk

1980s, USA, roller-printed synthetic

1920s, USA, screen-printed cotton

1970s, USA, roller-printed synthetic

1970s, USA, roller-printed synthetic

1930s, USA, roller-printed synthetic

1990s, USA, roller-printed synthetic

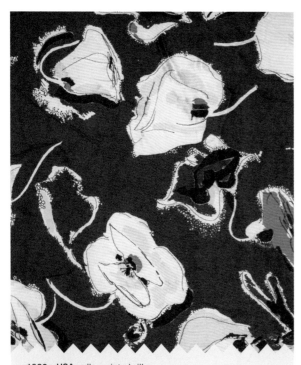

1930s, USA, roller-printed silk

1930s, USA, roller-printed synthetic

1970s, USA, roller-printed cotton

1970s, USA, roller-printed cotton

1963, France, roller-printed cotton

1990s, USA, roller-printed synthetic

1990s, France, roller-printed silk

1970s, USA, roller-printed synthetic

1970s, USA, roller-printed synthetic

c. 1967, USA, roller-printed cotton

c. 1970, USA, roller-printed cotton

1970s, USA, roller-printed synthetic

1950s, USA, roller-printed cotton

1990s, USA, roller-printed synthetic

1990s, USA, roller-printed synthetic

c. 1975, USA, roller-printed cotton

1990s, USA, roller-printed synthetic

c. 1925, USA, roller-printed cotton

1980s, USA, roller-printed cotton

1960s, USA, roller-printed cotton

1990s, USA, roller-printed silk

c. 1948, USA, roller-printed cotton

c. 1950, USA, roller-printed cotton

1870s, USA, roller-printed wool

1930s, USA, roller-printed synthetic

c. 1960, USA, roller-printed silk

c. 1968, Italy, roller-printed silk

1990s, USA, roller-printed synthetic

c. 1965, USA, roller-printed synthetic

1990s, USA, roller-printed synthetic

1920s, USA, roller-printed silk

1960s, USA, roller-printed cotton

1930s, USA, roller-printed synthetic

1910s, USA, roller-printed silk

1930s, USA, roller-printed silk

1930s, USA, roller-printed silk

c. 1968, Italy, roller-printed synthetic

1920s, Japan, roller-printed wool

1940s, USA, roller-printed cotton

c. 1970, USA, roller-printed synthetic

c. 1967, USA, roller-printed cotton

c. 1967, USA, roller-printed cotton

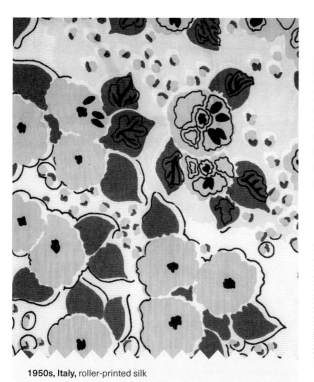

1950s, Italy, roller-printed silk

1990s, USA, roller-printed synthetic

1920s, USA, roller-printed silk

c. 1968, USA, roller-printed cotton

1950s, USA, roller-printed cotton

1940s, USA, roller-printed synthetic

1950s, USA, roller-printed cotton

c. 1960, USA, roller-printed cotton

1930s, USA, roller-printed synthetic

c. 1968, USA, roller-printed cotton

c. 1955, USA, roller-printed cotton

1850s, USA, roller-printed wool

1950s, USA, roller-printed synthetic

1990s, USA, roller-printed cotton

c. 1900, USA, roller-printed cotton

1840s, France, roller-printed wool

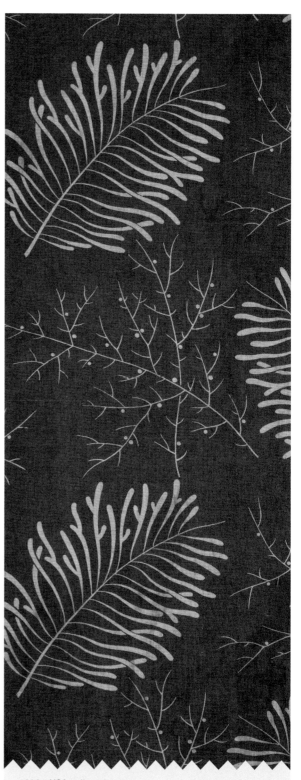

1890s, USA, roller-printed cotton

1840s, France, roller-printed silk and wool

1860s, France, roller-printed wool

1840s, France, roller-printed silk and wool

1890s, USA, roller-printed cotton

1880s, USA, roller-printed wool

1830s, France, roller-printed silk and wool

1830s, France, roller-printed silk and wool

1840s, France, roller-printed silk and wool

1930s, USA, roller-printed synthetic

1820s, France, roller-printed cotton

1850s, France, roller-printed silk and wool

1860s, France, roller-printed wool

1820s, USA, block-printed cotton

1990s, France, warp-printed silk

1990s, France, warp-printed silk

1870s, France, warp-printed silk

c. 1900, France, warp-printed silk

Chapter 2

Geometric

Chapter 2

Geometric

Lines, grids, circles, squares, triangles, and combinations of these elements, when arranged in neat or abstracted rows or columns, are inherently pleasing to the eye. This structure is so pleasing because it echoes geometric elements of the natural world: just picture seashells, plant structures, geological formations, and microscopic cellular structures.

It is no surprise, then, that geometric pattern has been a staple of decorative arts since the beginning of recorded time, evident in ancient Egyptian symbology and Greek and Roman architectural decorative motifs. However, it was the Art Deco period—which burst into being during the International Exhibition of Modern Decorative and Industrial Arts, held in Paris in 1925—that saw an explosion of new, modern ideas, and crisp elemental combinations. These ideas flourished in the ten to fifteen years following the exhibition and direct descendants of Art Deco are alive and well today—just see pages 78, 86, and 87.

As is usually the case, art and design are closely aligned, both pushing for progress and new forms of expression. How bizarre must the images from the Cubist art movement have appeared to the first audiences in the early twentieth century? The abstraction of figures, landscapes, and objects into their flat, base geometric shapes, colors, and shifting perspectives were revolutionary at the time, but have now become staples of our design vocabulary, continuing to provide a rich source of inspiration for pattern designers.

Modernism followed, cementing its aesthetic place at the table in the mid-twentieth century with designs that sought to break with classical and traditional forms. Post-World War II the world was in a fragile state, seeking a forward-thinking future. This instigated a rare moment in design evolution, in which designers did not look back longingly for inspiration but sought to smash everything old and begin anew. Still grappling with the devastation of the war and wary of technological advancements, most notably the creation of the atomic bomb, pattern designers took themes of "forward and new" and applied them to their craft. There are no historical designs that can be mistaken for the "atomic" pattern of the late 1940s and early 1950s. With intersecting lines, shapes, and atomic-like geometric structures, these patterns and images dominated the visual culture of this technologically rich era and pointed to a new, unrecognizable future.

Designers have continued to deconstruct, embellish, scale up and down, abstract, and reinterpret these ideas, creating a rich archive of geometric patterns that, despite all the variations in theme, color, and mood, still provide a framework for pattern design that pleases the eye and fulfils our desire for an orderly and organized visual world.

1940s–50s, USA,
roller-printed cotton

1970s–80s, USA, roller-printed synthetic

1970s–80s, USA, roller-printed synthetic

1970s–80s, USA, roller-printed synthetic

1970s–80s, USA, roller-printed synthetic

1970s–80s, USA, roller-printed synthetic

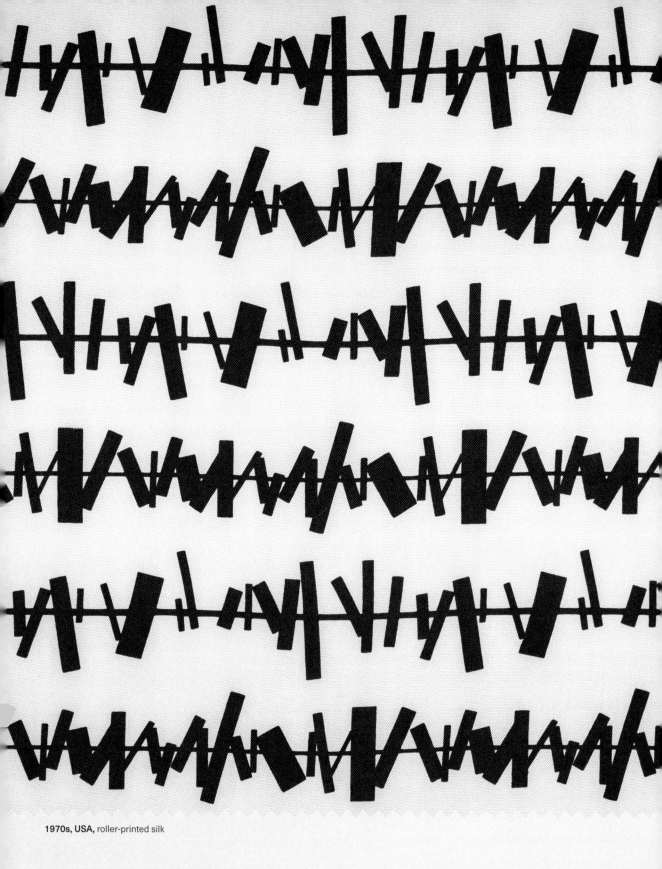

1970s, USA, roller-printed silk

1960s, USA, roller-printed synthetic

1970s, USA, roller-printed silk

1920s, USA, roller-printed silk

1920s, USA, roller-printed silk

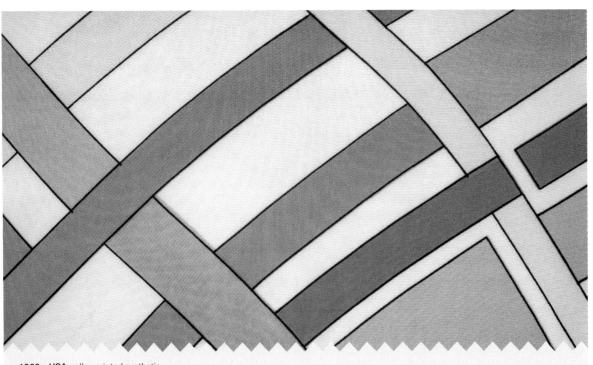

1960s, USA, roller-printed synthetic

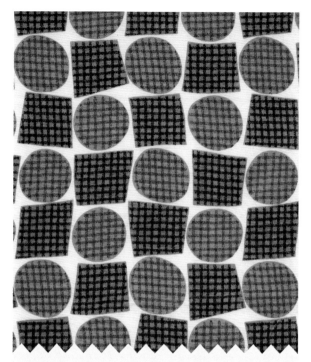

1950s, USA, roller-printed silk

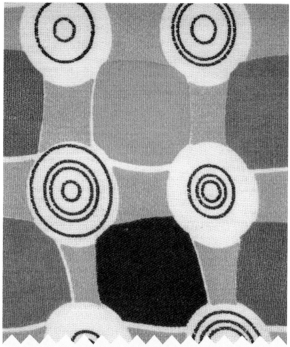

1940s, USA, roller-printed cotton

1910s, USA, roller-printed cotton

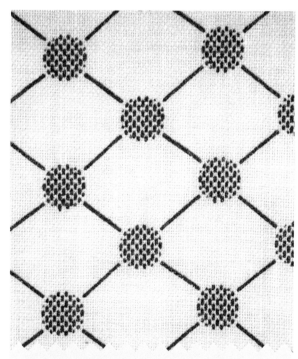

1870s, USA, roller-printed cotton

c. 1960, USA, roller-printed synthetic

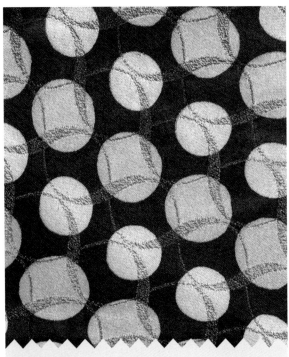

1920s, France, roller-printed silk

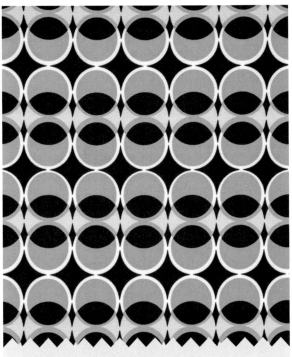

1870s, USA, roller-printed cotton

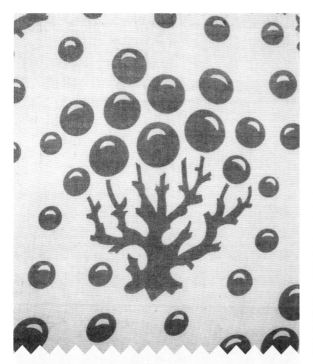

1920s, USA, roller-printed silk

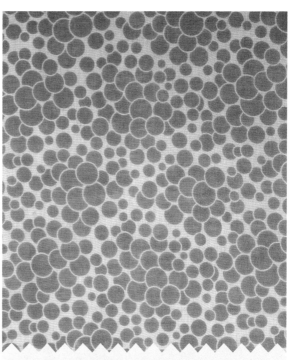

c. 1900, USA, roller-printed silk

c. 1970, USA, roller-printed synthetic

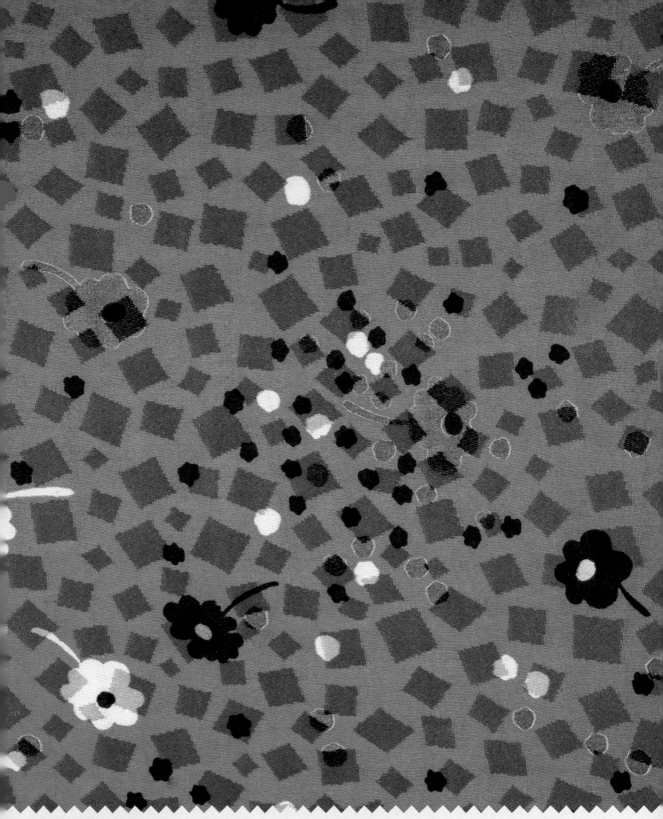

1930s, USA, roller-printed silk

1970s, USA, roller-printed synthetic

1980s, USA, roller-printed synthetic

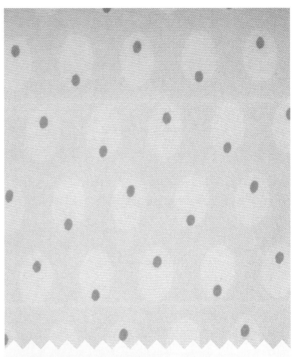

1970s, USA, roller-printed synthetic

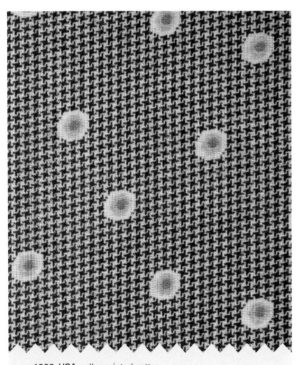

c. 1900, USA, roller-printed cotton

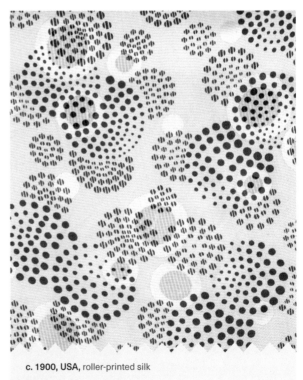

c. 1900, USA, roller-printed silk

c. 1950, USA, roller-printed cotton

c. 1967, USA, roller-printed synthetic

c. 1970, USA, screen-printed cotton

1970s, USA, roller-printed cotton

1970s–80s, USA, roller-printed synthetic

1970s, USA, roller-printed cotton

1970s, USA, screen-printed cotton

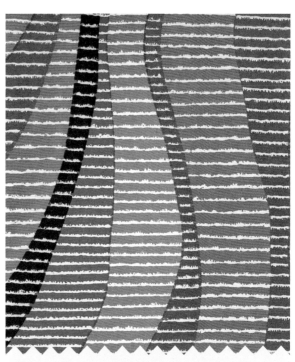

1970s, USA, screen-printed cotton

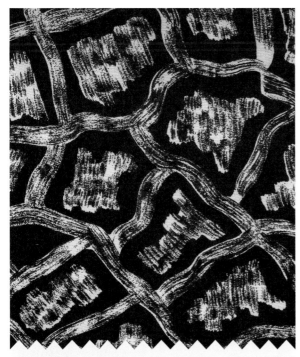

1950s, USA, roller-printed silk

c. 1985, France, roller-printed silk

c. 1960, USA, roller-printed synthetic

c. 1967, USA, roller-printed synthetic

1980s, USA, roller-printed synthetic

c. 1968, USA, screen-printed cotton

1940s–50s, USA, roller-printed cotton

1960s, USA, roller-printed cotton

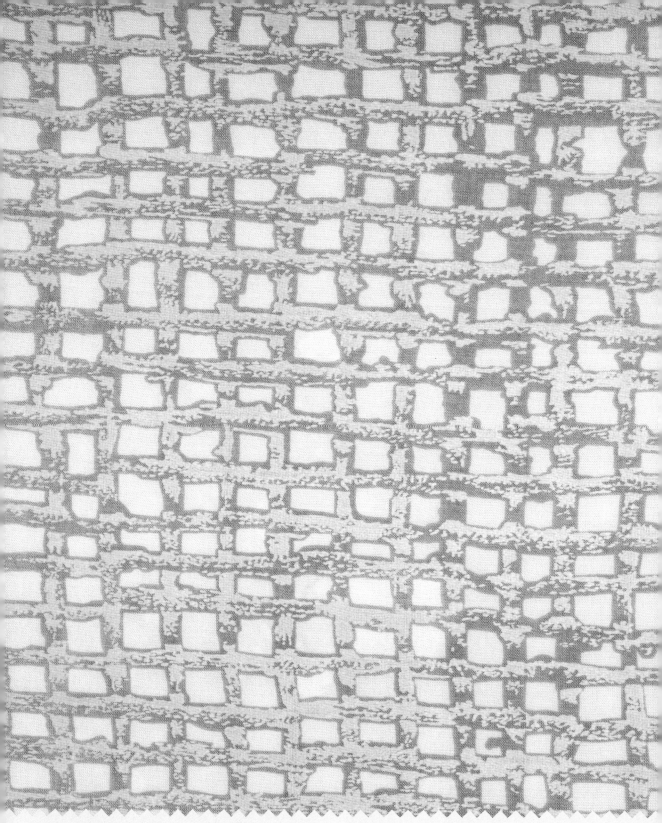

1950s, USA, roller-printed silk

1960s, USA, roller-printed cotton

c. 1948, USA, roller-printed silk

1930s, USA, roller-printed cotton

1910s, France, roller-printed silk

1970s, USA, roller-printed cotton

c. 1965, USA, screen-printed linen

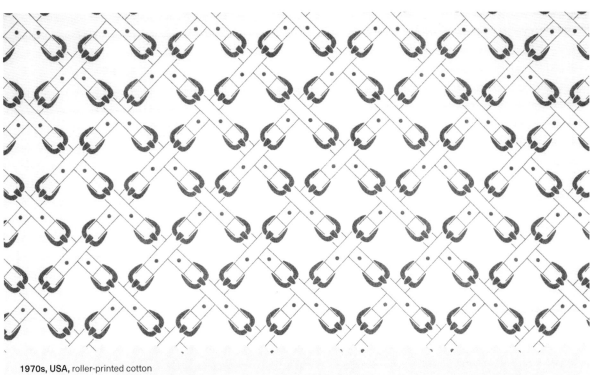

1970s, USA, roller-printed cotton

1960s, USA, roller-printed cotton

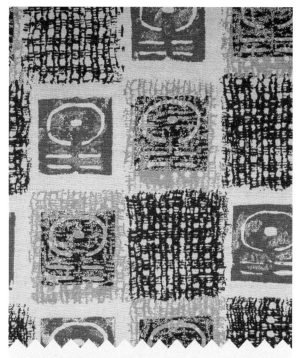

1940s–50s, USA, screen-printed cotton

1940s–50s, USA, roller-printed cotton

1940s–50s, USA, screen-printed cotton

1940s–50s, USA, screen-printed cotton

1940s–50s, USA, screen-printed cotton

c. 1973, USA, roller-printed synthetic

1860s, USA, roller-printed cotton

1950s, USA, roller-printed cotton

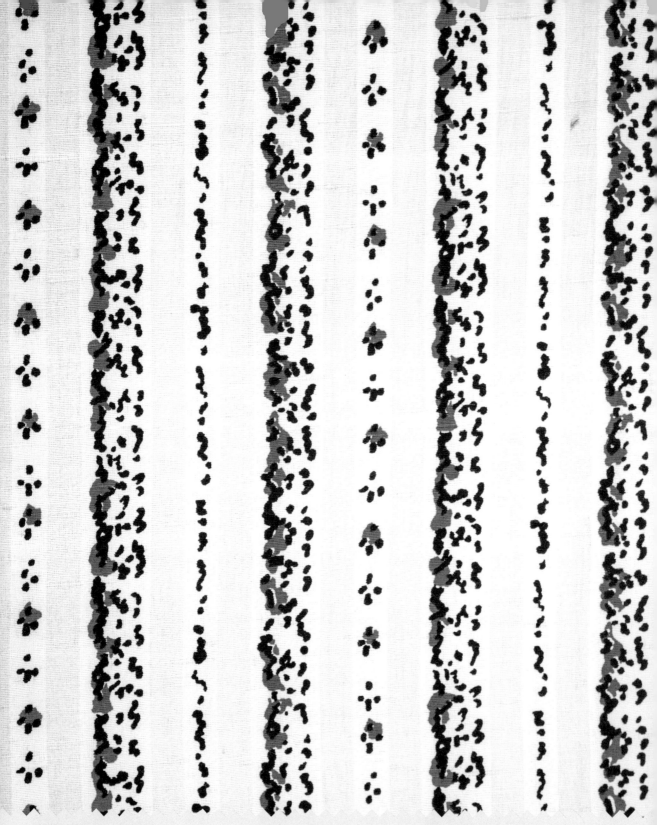

1940s, USA, roller-printed silk

1980s, Italy, roller-printed silk

1940s–50s, USA, roller-printed cotton

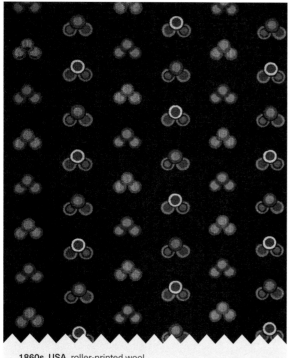

1860s, USA, roller-printed wool

1860s, USA, roller-printed wool

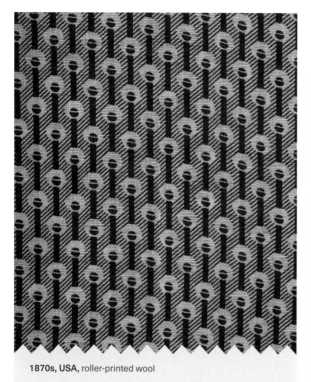

1870s, USA, roller-printed wool

1830s, USA, roller-printed cotton

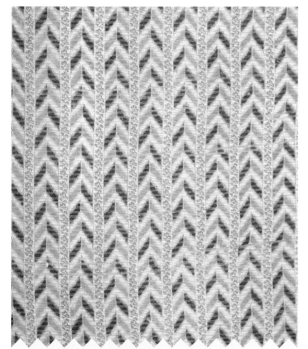

1840s, France, roller-printed silk and wool

1860s, USA, roller-printed cotton

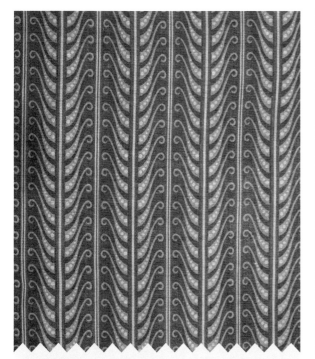

1840s, USA, roller-printed cotton

1870s, USA, roller-printed wool

1970s, USA, screen-printed cotton

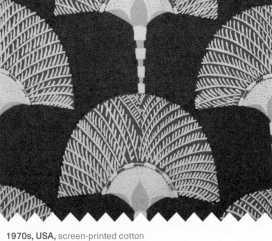

1980s, USA, roller-printed cotton

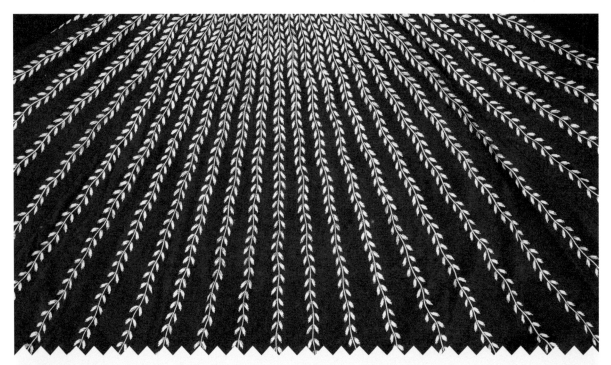

1950s, USA, roller-printed cotton

1890s, USA, roller-printed cotton

1890s, USA, roller-printed cotton

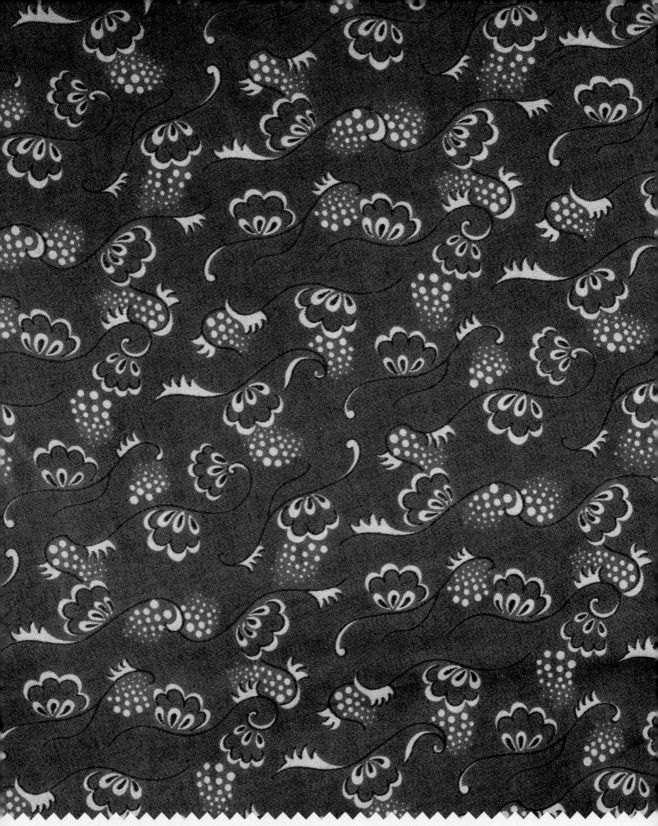

c. 1900–1905, USA, roller-printed silk

c. 1900–1905, USA, roller-printed silk

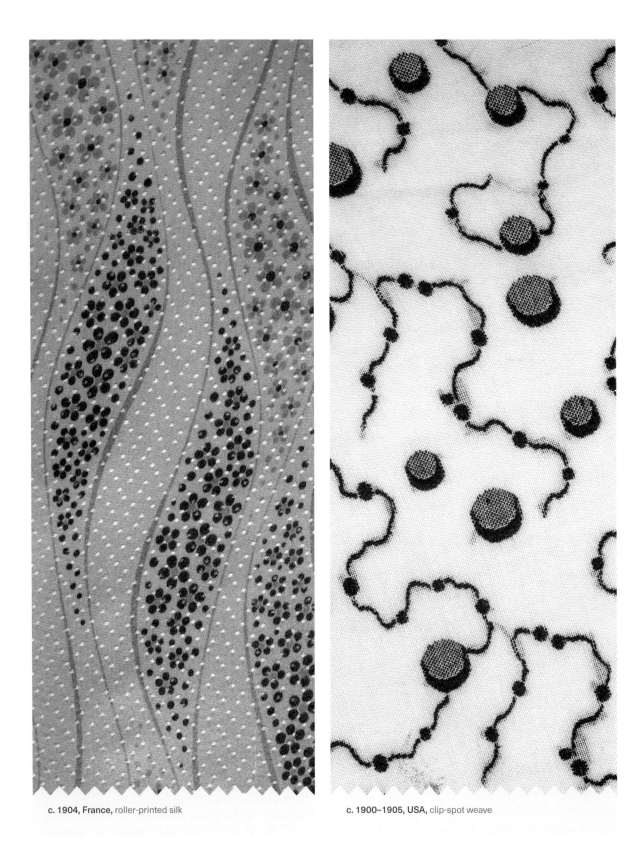

c. 1904, France, roller-printed silk

c. 1900–1905, USA, clip-spot weave

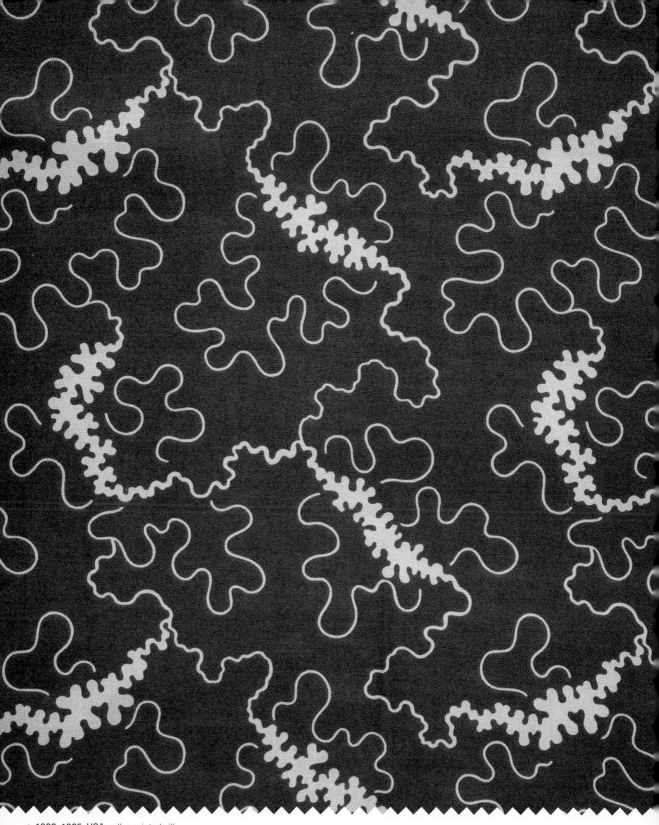

c. 1900–1905, USA, roller-printed silk

Chapter 3

Conversational

Conversational

We have Christophe-Philippe Oberkampf, a textile printer from just outside Versailles, France, to thank for the popularity of the conversational, or novelty, pattern. In the second half of the eighteenth century, Oberkampf created a textile pattern design, which, for the first time, featured tranquil bucolic scenes, full of farm animals, shepherds, and shepherdesses. These highly representational patterns, referred to as *toile de jouy*, began the trend for creating textile patterns infused with recognizable images of places or objects.

Conversational prints are whimsical and fun, and they've led to some wonderful patterns—and stories. In the first half of the twentieth century, for instance, manufacturers of chicken feed, flour, rice, beans—essentially anything sold in a cloth sack—realized that enterprising women were using their fabrics to create clothing. Sensing a marketing opportunity, these manufacturers hired textile designers to create cheerful prints, and used easily removable labels, so that women could choose from a wider range of patterns for their garments. A selection of these creations can be seen on pages 165 and 186.

Moments in popular culture have also inspired textile print ideas. When television was still in its infancy, Westerns showcasing the Wild West of America, with gunslingers and cowboys, were incredibly popular. Textile creators harnessed this iconography, creating Western-infused prints for both garments and interiors. This was also the case for the colorful clown. Children's television programming usually included some form of friendly and instructive clown, and so it is hardly surprising that this figure, and all the characters found in the circus, would make their way to textiles such as those on pages 138–141. Similarly, the 1970s saw renewed interest in the Victorian cheater quilt (see pages 161–163), a textile form of *trompe l'œil*, which was created to resemble many small patches carefully stitched together by hand, but with none of the effort!

In America, national pride proved another popular subject. There was a flurry of prints developed in the lead-up to the bicentennial anniversary, in 1976, of the founding of America. In these commemorative patterns, colonial artifacts, figures in historic costume, and references to the beginnings of a nation were all used in profusion to create vignettes and dioramic scenes.

Though not always tasteful, conversational prints are fun snapshots of the times in which they were created.

c. 1950, USA, roller-printed synthetic

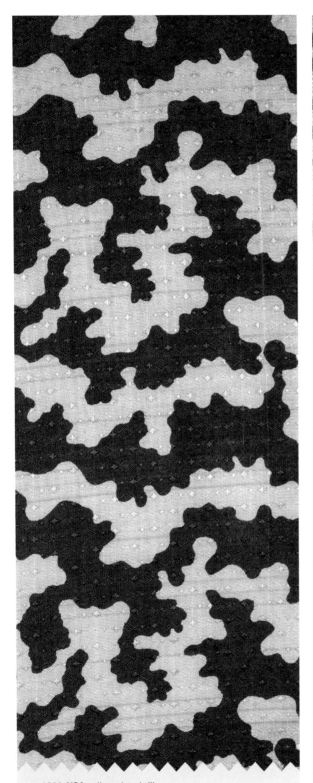

c. 1900, USA, roller-printed silk

1930s, USA, roller-printed synthetic

1940s–50s, USA, roller-printed wool

1940s–50s, USA, roller-printed silk

1940s–50s, USA, roller-printed synthetic

c. 1949, USA, roller-printed synthetic

1940s, USA, roller-printed synthetic

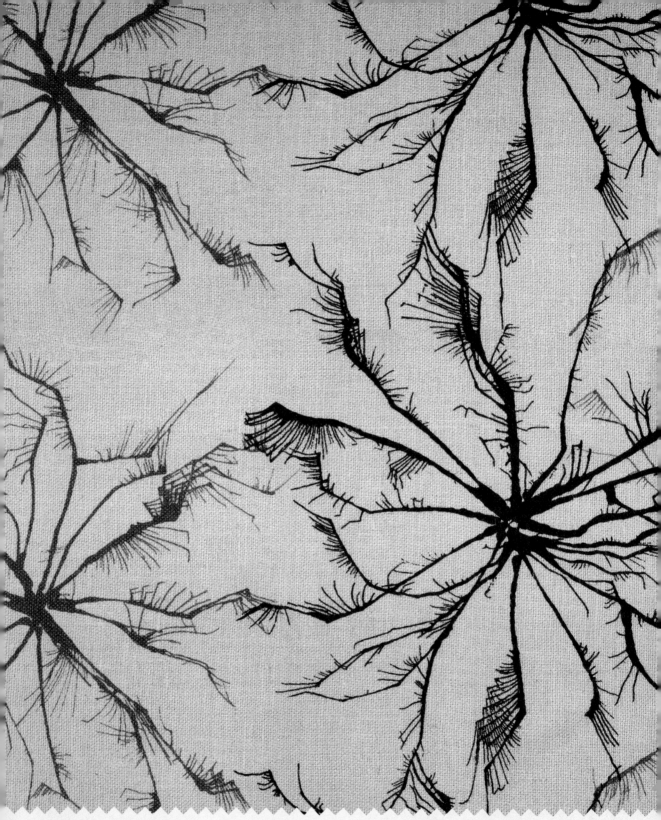

1960s, USA, screen-printed linen

c. 1980, France, roller-printed cotton

1940s, USA, roller-printed synthetic

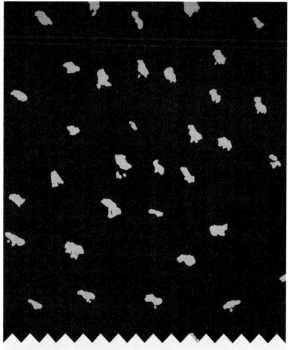

1950s, USA, roller-printed silk

1950s, USA, roller-printed cotton

1960s, USA, roller-printed cotton

1960s, USA, roller-printed cotton

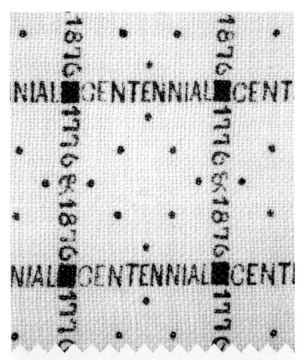

c. 1876, USA, roller-printed cotton (detail)

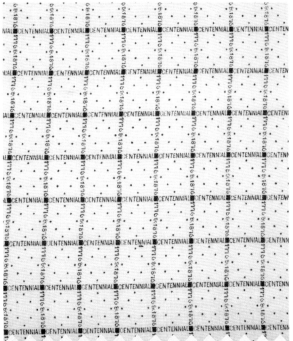

c. 1876, USA, roller-printed cotton

1950s, USA, roller-printed or screen-printed cotton

1960s, USA, roller-printed cotton

1970s, USA, roller-printed cotton

1990s, USA, roller-printed synthetic

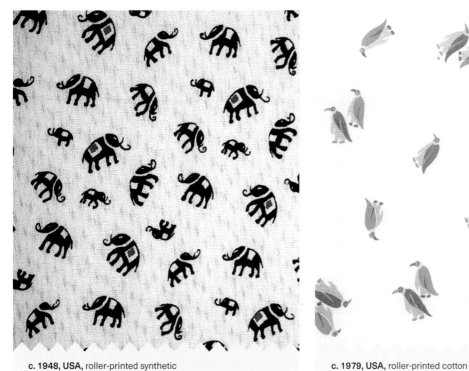

c. 1948, USA, roller-printed synthetic

c. 1979, USA, roller-printed cotton

1970s, USA, roller-printed cotton

1940s, USA, roller-printed cotton

1970s, USA, roller-printed synthetic

1910

1905

1907

1912

1912

1910

1908

1912

1909

1907

1960s, USA, roller-printed cotton

c. 1943, USA, roller-printed synthetic

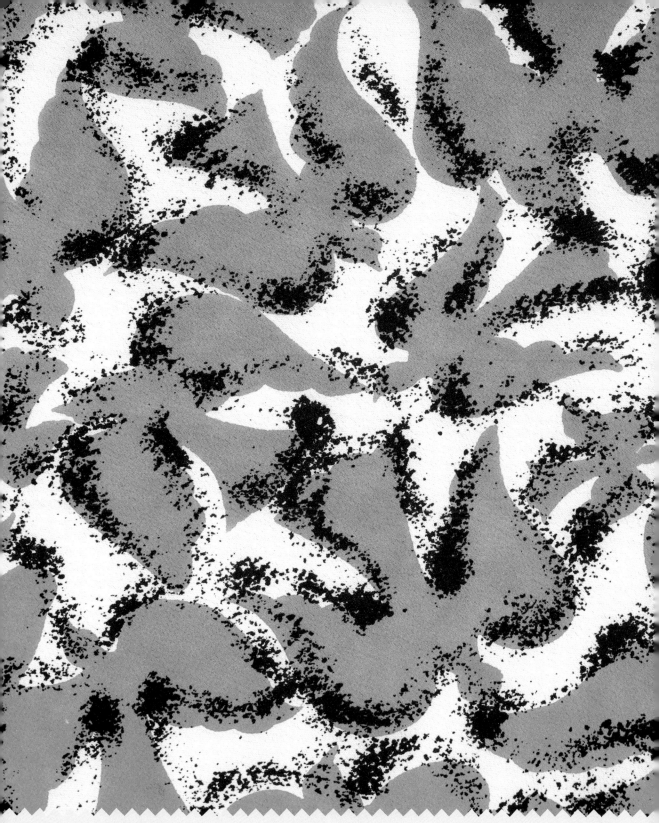

1950s, USA, roller-printed synthetic

1920s, Japan, roller-printed silk

1940s–50s, USA, screen-printed linen

c. 1975, USA, roller-printed cotton-synthetic blend

c. 1975, USA, roller-printed cotton-synthetic blend

c. 1960, USA, roller-printed cotton

c. 1955, USA, roller-printed cotton

1930s, USA, roller-printed cotton

1930s, USA, roller-printed cotton

1950s, USA, jacquard weave silk

1980s, USA, roller-printed cotton

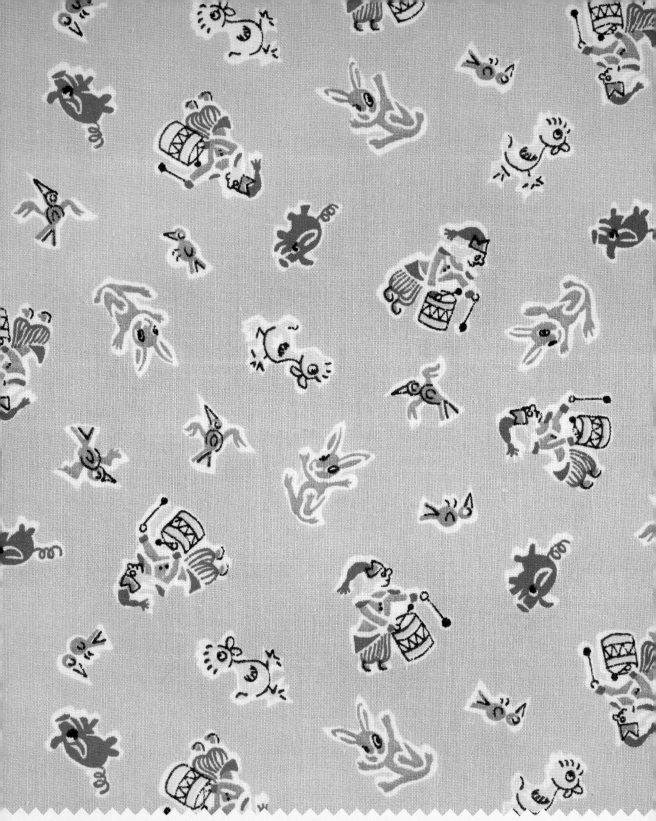

1930s, USA, roller-printed cotton

1960s, USA, roller-printed cotton

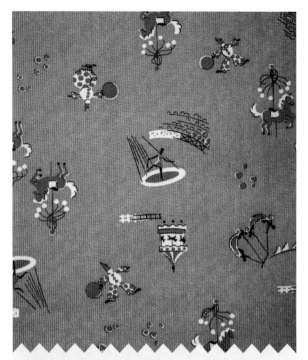

1950s, USA, roller-printed cotton

c. 1970, USA, roller-printed cotton

1950s, USA, roller-printed cotton

1990s, France, roller-printed synthetic

1960s, USA, roller-printed cotton

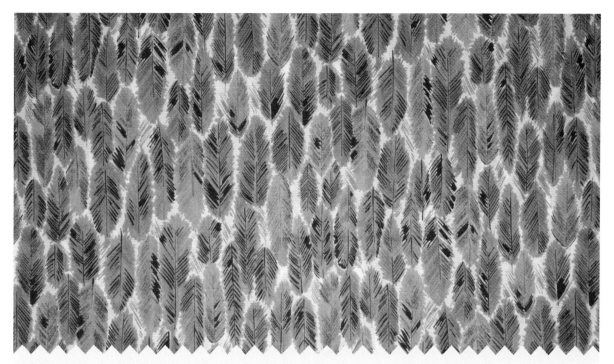

1960s, USA, roller-printed silk

1980s, Italy, roller-printed synthetic

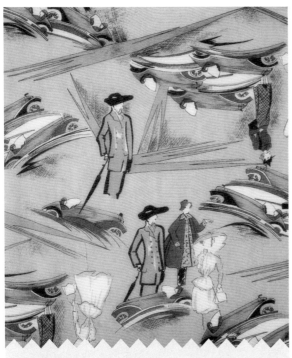

1970s, USA, roller-printed synthetic

c. 1965, USA, roller-printed cotton

c. 1948, USA, roller-printed silk

1950s, USA, roller-printed silk

1980s, France, screen-printed cotton

c. 1960, USA, roller-printed cotton

1940s, USA, roller-printed synthetic

1970s, USA, roller-printed synthetic

1990s, USA, roller-printed cotton

1950s, USA, roller-printed silk

1940s, USA, roller-printed synthetic

1990s, USA, roller-printed silk

c. 1960, USA, roller-printed cotton

1970s, USA, roller-printed synthetic

1970s, USA, roller-printed cotton-synthetic blend

1970s, USA, screen-printed vinyl

c. 1950, USA, roller-printed synthetic

c. 1967, USA, roller-printed cotton

1960s, Germany, roller-printed wool

1980s, USA, roller-printed cotton

1930s, USA, roller-printed silk

1930s, USA, roller-printed cotton

1980s, USA, roller-printed synthetic

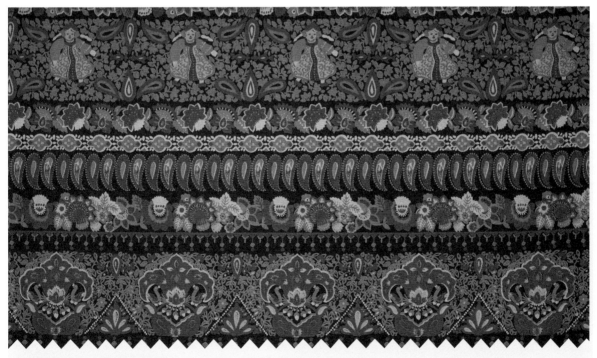

1980s, USA, roller-printed synthetic

1980s, USA, roller-printed cotton

c. 1968, USA, roller-printed cotton

1930s, USA, roller-printed silk

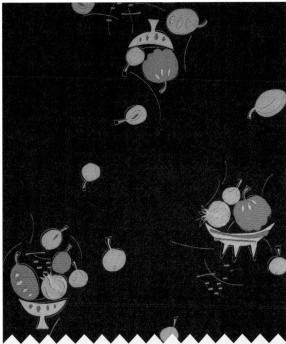

c. 1955, USA, roller-printed cotton

c. 1973, USA, roller-printed cotton

1930s, USA, roller-printed cotton

1920s, USA, roller-printed silk

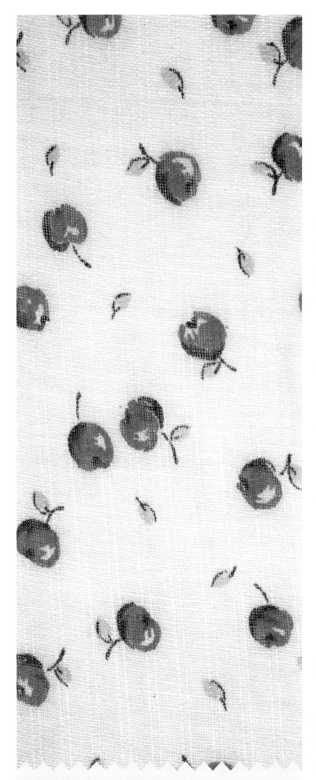

1850s, USA, roller-printed cotton

1980s, Italy, roller-printed or silk screen-printed cotton

1970s, USA, roller-printed synthetic

1970s, USA, roller-printed cotton

1970s, USA, roller-printed cotton

1970s, USA, roller-printed cotton

1970s, USA, roller-printed cotton

1970s, USA, roller-printed cotton

c. 1955, USA, roller-printed cotton

1940s, USA, roller-printed cotton

1870s, USA, roller-printed wool

1940s, USA, roller-printed cotton

c. 1970, USA, roller-printed cotton

c. 1980, USA, roller-printed cotton

c. 1960, USA, roller-printed cotton

1970s, USA, roller-printed cotton

1970s, USA, screen-printed cotton

USA, 1970s, roller-printed cotton

1980s, USA, roller-printed synthetic

1980s, USA, screen-printed silk

1950s, USA, roller-printed cotton

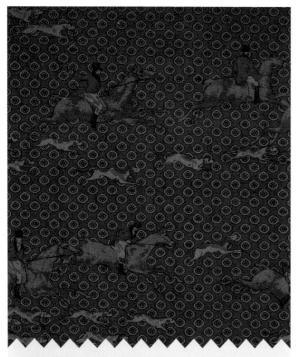

1980s, USA, roller-printed synthetic

1980s, USA, roller-printed synthetic

1950s, USA, roller-printed cotton

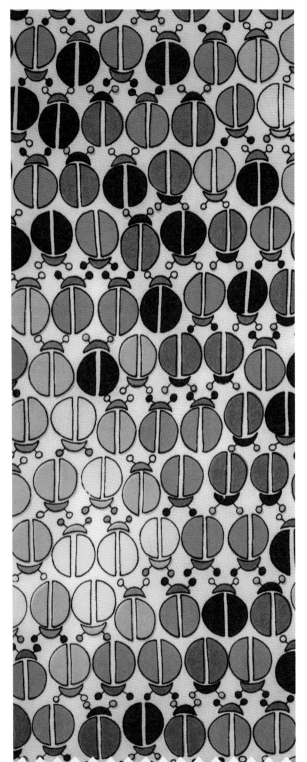

c. 1970, USA, roller-printed synthetic

c. 1975, USA, screen-printed cotton

c. 1973, USA, roller-printed cotton-synthetic blend

c. 1995, USA, screen-printed silk

1940s, USA, roller-printed cotton

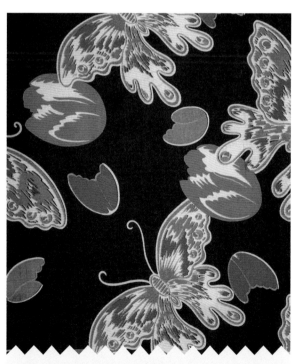

1930s, USA, roller-printed synthetic

1940s, USA, roller-printed cotton

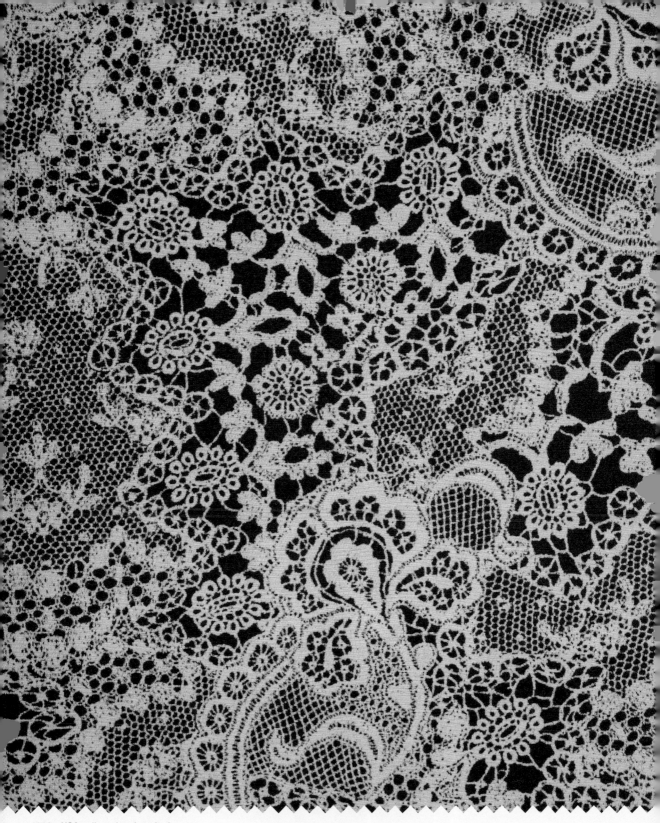

1980s, USA, roller-printed synthetic

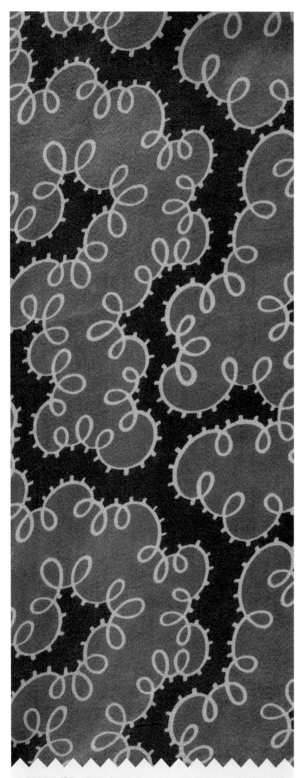

1890s, USA, roller-printed silk

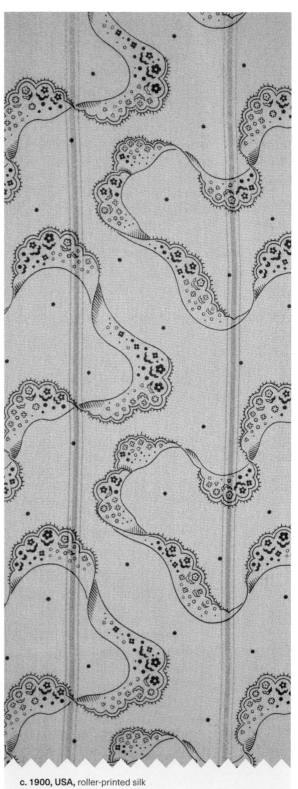

c. 1900, USA, roller-printed silk

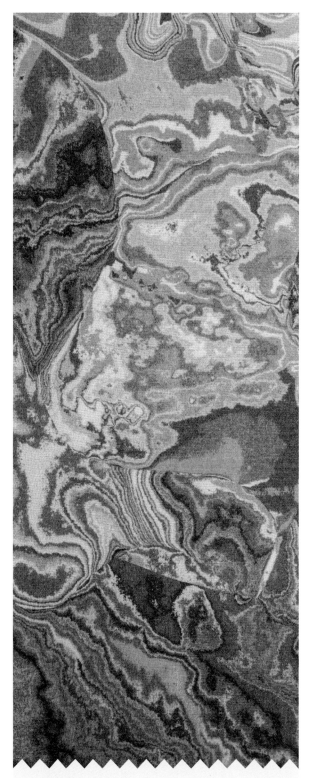

c. 1968, USA, roller-printed synthetic

1990s, USA, roller-printed synthetic

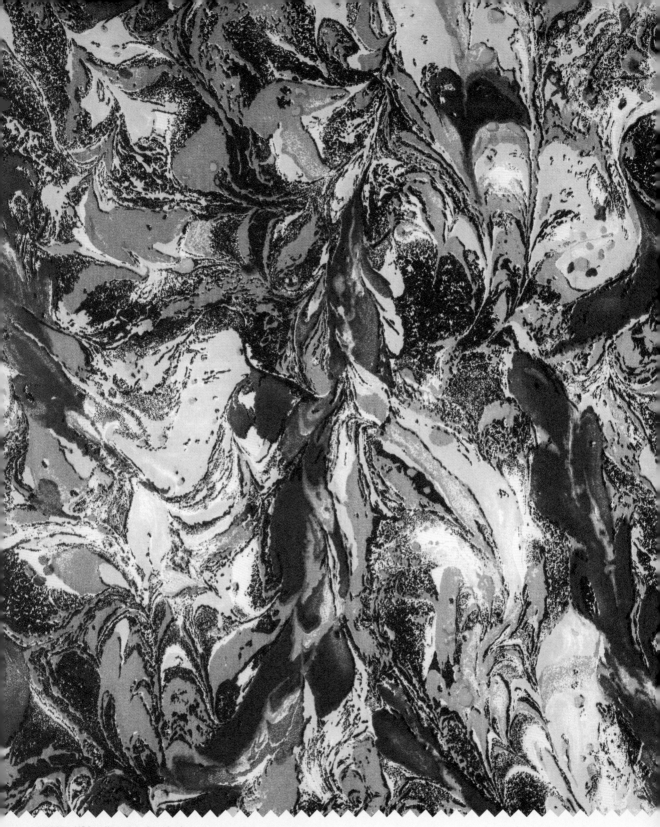

1960s, USA, roller-printed synthetic

1960s, USA, roller-printed synthetic

1970s, USA, screen-printed cotton

1970s, USA, roller-printed cotton

c. 1980, USA, roller-printed cotton

c. 1970, USA, screen-printed cotton

1970s, USA, roller-printed synthetic

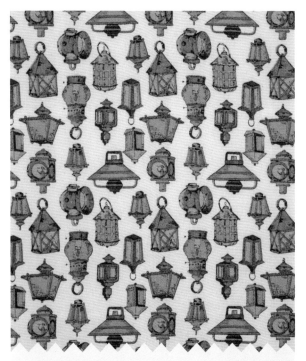

1950s, USA, roller-printed cotton

1960s, USA, screen-printed cotton

1950s, USA, roller-printed cotton

1960s, USA, roller-printed cotton

c. 1960, USA, screen-printed cotton

1940s, USA, roller-printed cotton

c. 1950, USA, roller-printed cotton

c. 1944, USA, roller-printed synthetic

1960s, USA, roller-printed cotton

1960s, USA, roller-printed synthetic

c. 1995, USA, roller-printed cotton

1950s, USA, roller-printed cotton

1950s, USA, roller-printed cotton

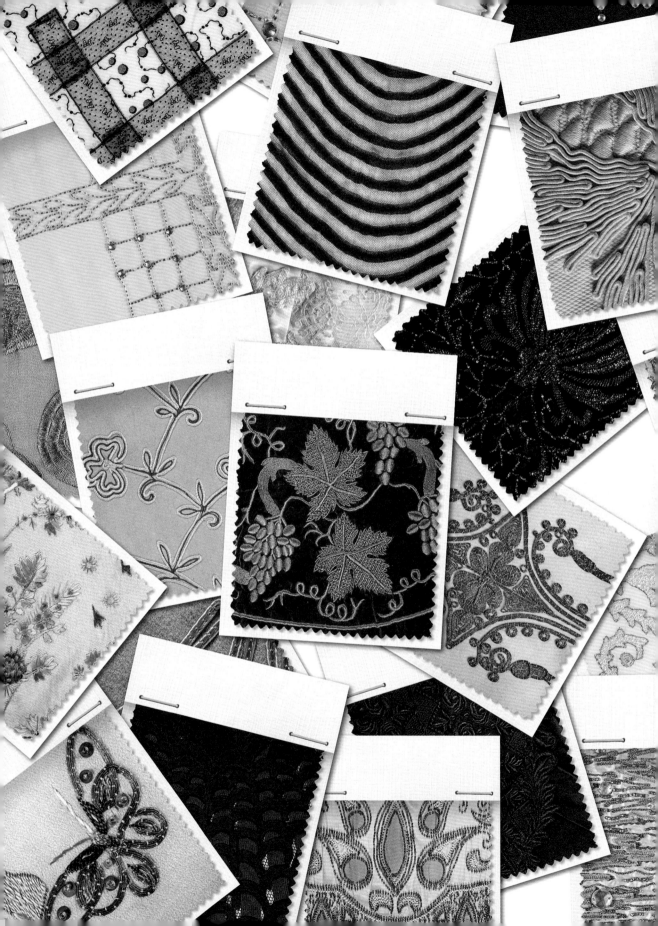

Chapter 4

Constructed
Pattern

Applied
Beaded
Braid
Embroidery
Pierced

Chapter 4

Constructed Pattern

Before the Industrial Revolution, highly decorative garments were the domain of the very wealthy, markers of wealth and social standing. The rise of factory manufacturing, however, democratized textile design like never before, as sequenced assembly lines replaced skilled artisans working by hand. By the 1880s, virtually every decorative trim, braid, bead, ornament, or button imaginable was available and could be easily produced. The results were lush, layered, lace-encrusted, and die-cut textile designs in ready-to-wear quantities, at a fraction of the cost.

The most common trims used to create these decorative applied patterns were machine-woven braids, such as soutache and middy braid. These braids had 360 degrees of flexibility, which meant they could be stitched into very tight curves and used to create wonderfully complex patterns. Soutache, also known as Russian or tracing braid, is created by weaving a decorative thread around and between two parallel cords. It is typically ⅛ inch wide and has an indentation down the center, between the two cords, that makes a natural track for stitch application—which, by the end of the nineteenth century, was increasingly done using a sewing machine. Middy braid is flat and ¼ inch wide and is useful for simpler applications. It can also

be stitched down on just one edge of the braid, leaving the other edge to float free, creating a more three-dimensional surface. This effect can be seen on pages 203–219.

The Industrial Revolution also simplified the creation of gossamer lace trims, making it possible to purchase massive quantities at low prices. These beautiful machine-made varieties could then be applied in profusion onto a base fabric, creating pleasing applied patterns like those on page 247.

At this time, some of the most elaborately constructed, multi-layered textile designs started with a base layer of decoratively pierced wool felt. Each element of a pattern would be made into a sharp metal die shape that would be placed over the felt. Hydraulic force would then be applied to press the die through the material, piercing out the patterns. The pierced felt would then often be layered over other textural materials, such as lace, before braid, beads, and embroidery were applied on top. These sumptuous creations can be seen on pages 229–231.

The Industrial Revolution, therefore, shaped the textile and fashion industries in a way that celebrated the innovative spirit of the nineteenth century, and gave us some of the most fantastic examples of what can be achieved when art and design embrace technology.

1910s, USA,
couched braid and
machine topstitching
on wool

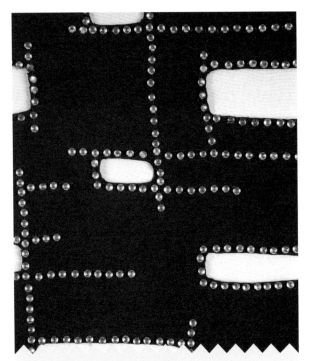

1920s, USA, metallic-studded silk with faced openings

1920s, USA, appliqué embroidered squares on silk

c. 1900, USA, stitched bias bands on silk

1900–1905, USA, insertion lace on cotton

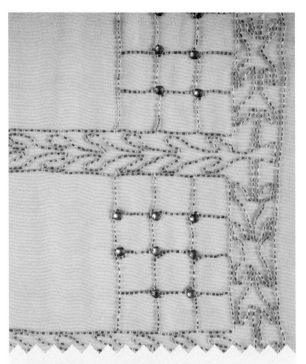

1920s, USA, glass beads and rhinestone studs on silk

1920s, USA, glass beads and rhinestone studs on silk

1870s, USA, beading and appliqué on silk

1890s, USA, glass beads on silk

1890s, USA, glass beads on silk

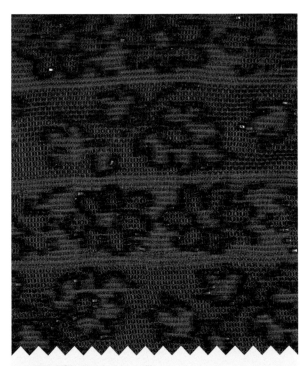

1890s, USA, glass beads on silk

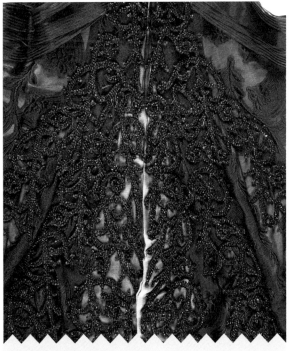

1890s, USA, glass beads on silk

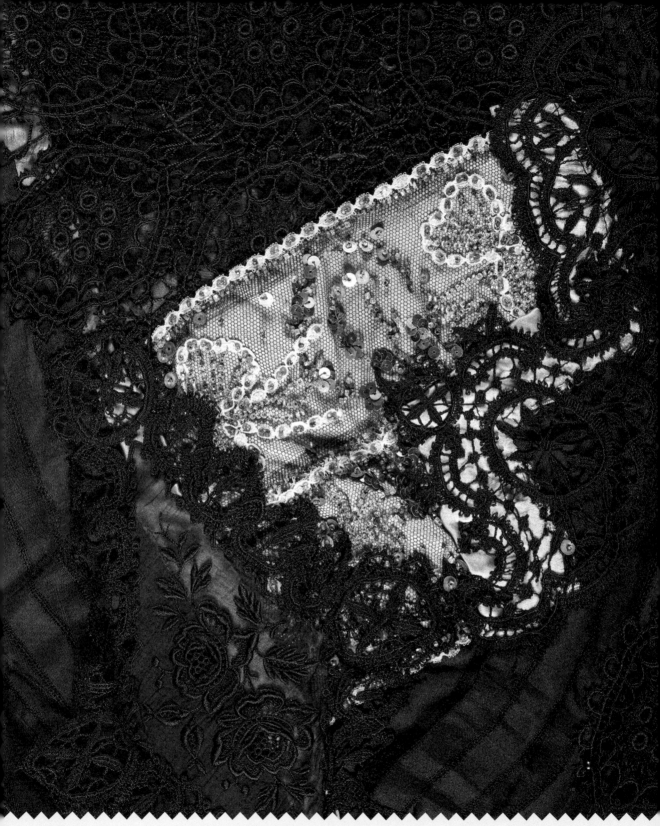

1900–1905, USA, glass beads and sequins on silk

1890s, USA, glass beads on silk

1890s, USA, glass beads on silk

1910s, USA, glass beads on silk

1880s, USA, glass beads on silk

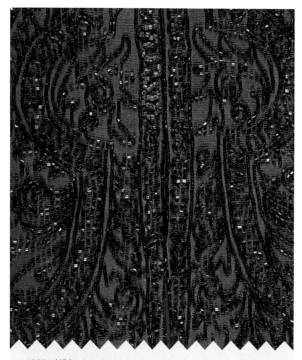

1880s, USA, glass beads on silk

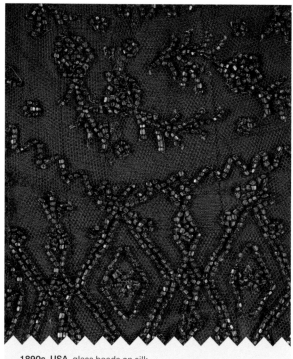

1890s, USA, glass beads on silk

1880s, USA, glass beads on silk

1880s, USA, glass beads on silk

1900–1905, **France,** embroidery and soutache braid on cotton

1890s, Turkey, couched metallic braid on wool

1890s, Turkey, couched braid on wool

1904, France, soutache braid on wool

1880s, USA, soutache braid and embroidery on wool

1890s, Turkey, couched metallic braid on wool

1890s, Turkey, couched metallic braid on wool

1900–1905, France, soutache braid and embroidery on cotton

1900–1905, France, soutache braid and embroidery on cotton

1890s, Turkey, couched metallic braid on wool

1890s, Turkey, couched metallic braid on wool

1910s, USA, soutache braid and satin cord on silk

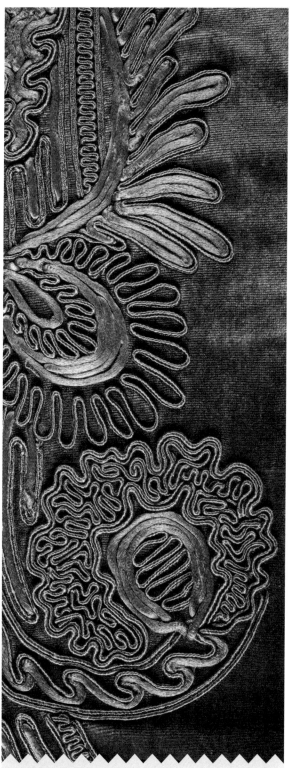

1910s, USA, soutache braid and satin cord on silk

1890s, Turkey, couched metallic braid on wool

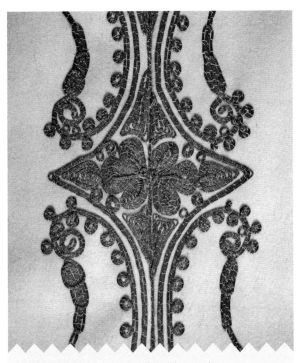

1890s, Turkey, couched metallic braid on wool

1890s, USA, round cord on linen

1880s, USA, soutache braid on cotton

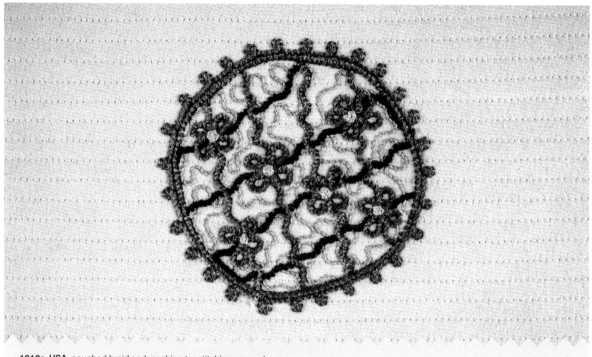

1910s, USA, couched braid and machine topstitching on wool

1910s, USA, couched braid and machine topstitching on wool

c. 1905, USA, soutache and middy braids on wool

c. 1905, USA, soutache braid on wool

c. 1909, USA, round cord on silk

1910s, USA, couched soutache braid on wool

1910s, USA, soutache braid and satin cord on silk

c. 1900, USA, flat braid and ruched ribbon on silk

1920s, USA, flat braid and embroidery on wool

c. 1910, USA, soutache braid and embroidery on silk

1880s, USA, soutache braid and round cord on wool

1880s, USA, soutache braid and round cord on wool

1880s, USA, soutache braid and round cord on wool

1880s, USA, soutache braid on wool

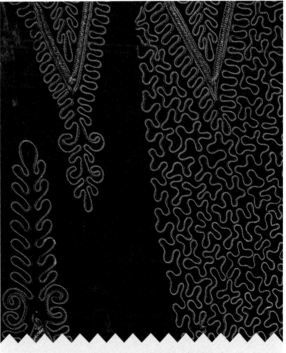

1880s, USA, soutache braid and round cord on wool

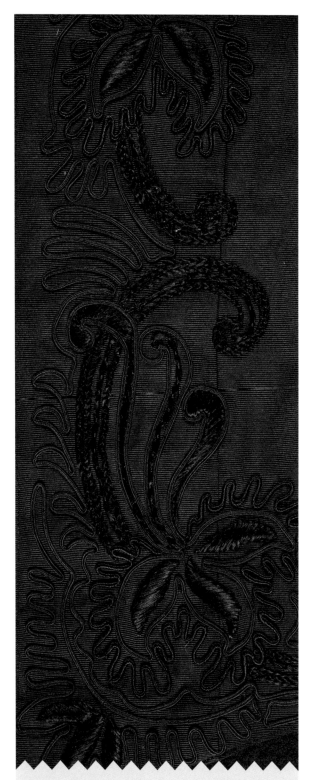

1890s, USA, soutache braid and appliqué on silk

c. 1900, USA, soutache, flat braids, and embroidery on silk

c. 1900, USA, soutache, flat braids, and embroidery on silk

1890s, USA, soutache and flat braids on wool

1890s, USA, soutache braid, round cord, and embroidery on silk

c. 1820, USA, embroidered silk

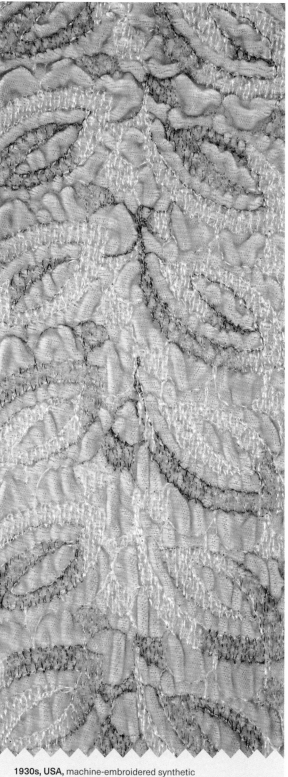

1930s, USA, machine-embroidered synthetic

1880s, France, straw braid and embroidery on silk

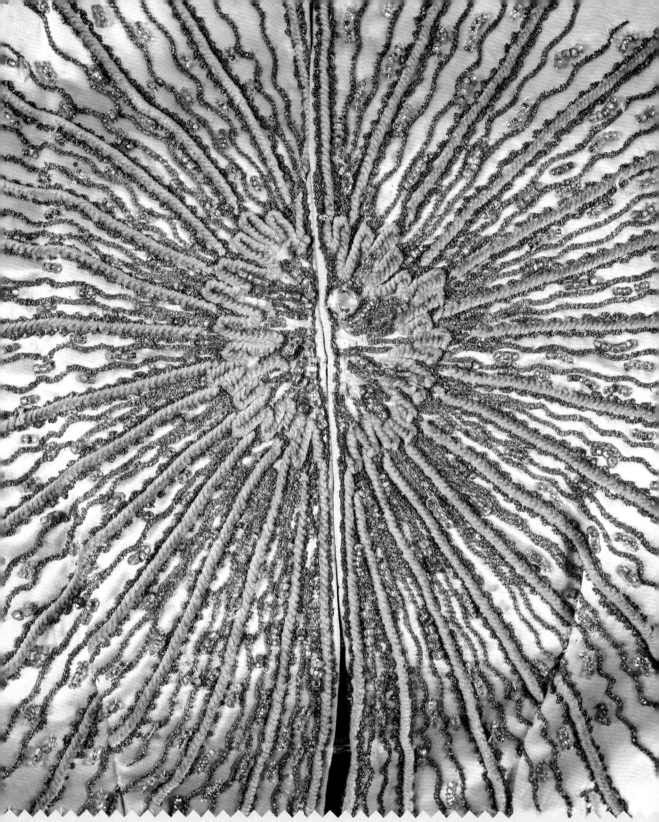

1930s, USA, round cord, glass beads, and embroidery on silk

1930s, USA, round cord, glass beads, and embroidery on silk

1920s, USA, glass beads on machine-embroidered silk

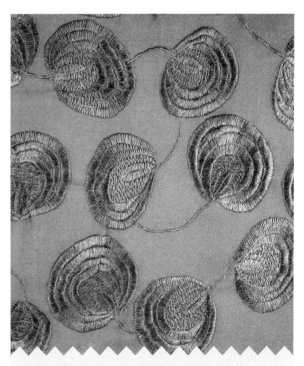

1920s, USA, glass beads on machine-embroidered silk

c. 1910, **China,** round cord, glass beads, and embroidery on silk

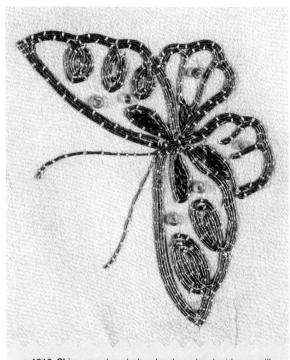

c. 1910, **China,** round cord, glass beads, and embroidery on silk

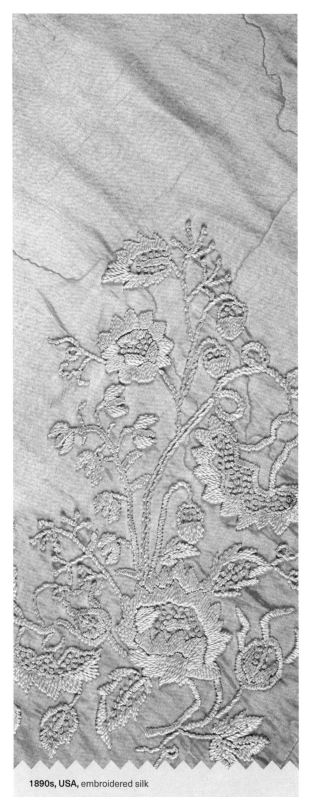

1890s, **USA,** embroidered silk

c. 1905, USA, embroidered appliqué on silk

c. 1910, USA, embroidered linen

1840s, USA, embroidered silk

1910s, USA, machine-embroidered silk

c. 1900, USA, flat braid and embroidery on silk

1920s, China, couched metallic cord on silk

1920s, France, embroidery embellished with sewn-on pronged rhinestones on silk

c. 1900, USA, pierced wool felt, soutache braid, and lace

c. 1900, USA, pierced wool felt, soutache braid, and lace

1890s, USA, pierced worsted wool, soutache braid, and round cord

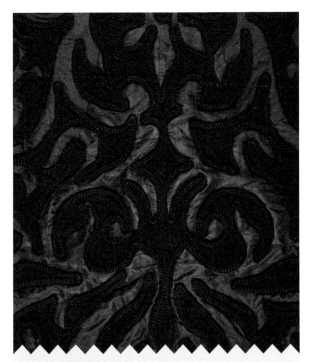

1890s, USA, pierced worsted wool, flat braid, and appliqué

1890s, USA, pierced wool felt and flat braid on net

1890s, USA, pierced wool felt, glass beads, and sequins

Chapter 5

Brocade

Chapter 5
Brocade

Patterns are not always printed or applied to material; some of the most beautiful examples are woven directly into the fabric during its creation. This is not driven by a functional need—this decoration could simply be printed onto the surface—but the human desire to challenge ourselves through complexity. Brocade is a perfect example of this need.

With its smooth, shiny, monofilament fiber, silk is an obvious choice for weaving complex brocade patterns. The Chinese were the first to harness its potential, in c. AD 960, guarding the technique from the West for thousands of years. As their creations worked their way along the Silk Road, passing through Byzantium, people began to wonder about this wonderful fiber and the elaborate weaves it created.

By the fourth century, the West had produced complex draw looms. These looms required two people to operate them: a weaver and a draw boy, who lifted the correct warp threads when instructed to by the weaver. But, while this loom produced brocade designs of wool and linen, silk remained a Chinese mystery. It wasn't until the sixth century that the Chinese secrets of sericulture (silk farming) were unveiled to the Byzantine empire, and silk production could begin in the Western world. The earliest brocade-woven patterns using silk were, unsurprisingly, created for the Church, and so Christian-themed motifs predominated. As the industry spread into Italy, then France, and eventually into England, however, the motifs became more decorative, incorporating precious metallic threads, along with areas of pile or velvet.

Because of this unabashed luxury, brocades were an indicator of status and wealth.

It finally became more accessible in 1804 when the Frenchman Joseph Marie Jacquard developed a system of punch cards that could be attached to the draw loom to speed up the process of brocade weaving. This system replaced the tedious task of the draw boy, which in turn increased production, reduced cost, and thus made woven brocade available to a wider audience.

Then, in the 1880s, under the strict eye of the English-born French couturier Charles Worth, brocade once again came to the fore, as women's fashion looked to the eighteenth-century French court as style inspiration. Worth's designs used heavy brocades adorned with elaborate rococo patterns that were last seen in the court of Marie Antoinette. Some wonderful examples of these nineteenth-century brocades are found on page 247.

Another moment of brocade-fever came in 1968, when Franco Zeffirelli enchanted the world with his film *Romeo and Juliet*, in which the beautiful leads wore heavy brocades and satins. By this time synthetic fibers were available, as were light-catching metallic-impersonating threads made from mylar and plastics. Woven in a 1960s color palette, these textiles, such as those on pages 248–251, created a fresh, modern twist on traditional brocades.

However, as fashion and fabrics softened over time, the popularity of these stiff brocades waned, and they were consigned once again to the area of home furnishings.

1850s, France,
silk

1880s, France, silk

1850s, France, silk

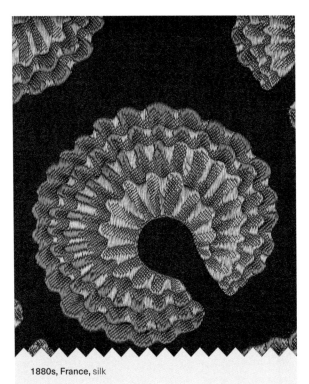

1880s, France, silk

1880s, France, silk

1880s, France, silk

1880s, France, silk

1880s, France, silk

1920s, France, silk

1880s, France, silk

1850s, France, silk

1920s, France, silk

1920s, France, silk

1926, France, silk and metallic yarns

1920s, France, silk and metallic yarns

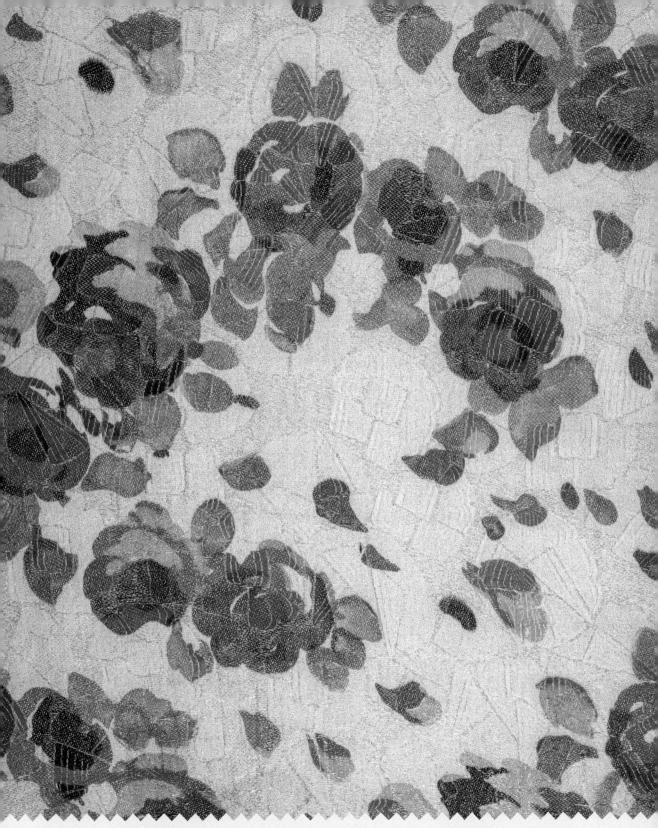

1920s, France, silk and metallic yarns

1920s, France, silk and metallic yarns

1920s, France, silk and metallic yarns

1920s, China, silk and metallic yarns

1920s, France, silk and metallic yarns

1890s, France, silk

1950s, France, silk and cotton

1850s, France, silk

1860s, France, silk

1840s, France, silk

1850s, France, silk

1960s, France, silk and metallic yarns

1960s, USA, synthetic and metallic yarns

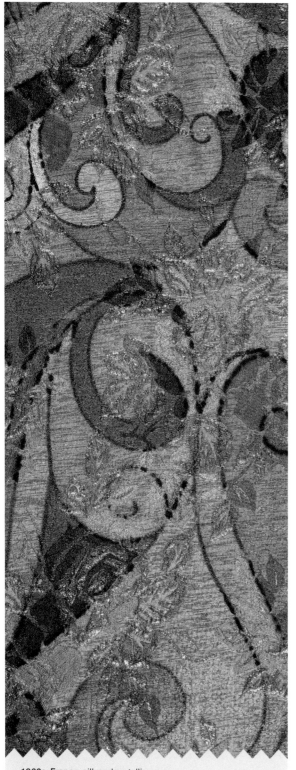

1960s, **France,** silk and metallic yarns

1960s, **USA,** synthetic

1960s, **France,** silk

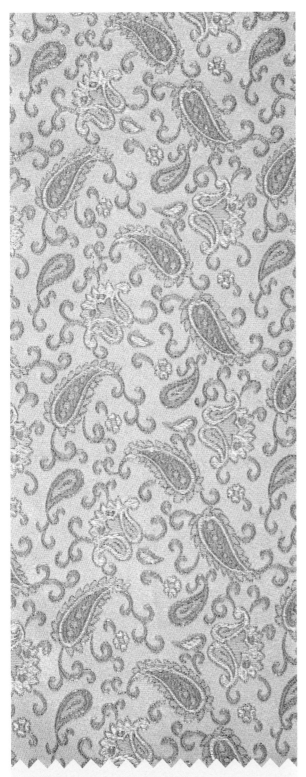

1960s, USA, synthetic and metallic yarns

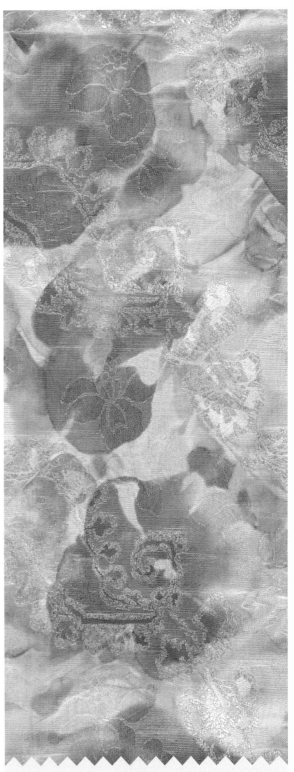

1990s, France, silk and metallic yarns

1870s, France, silk

1890s, France, silk

c. 1900, France, silk

1910s, France, silk

1890s, France, silk

1910s, France, silk

c. 1900, France, silk

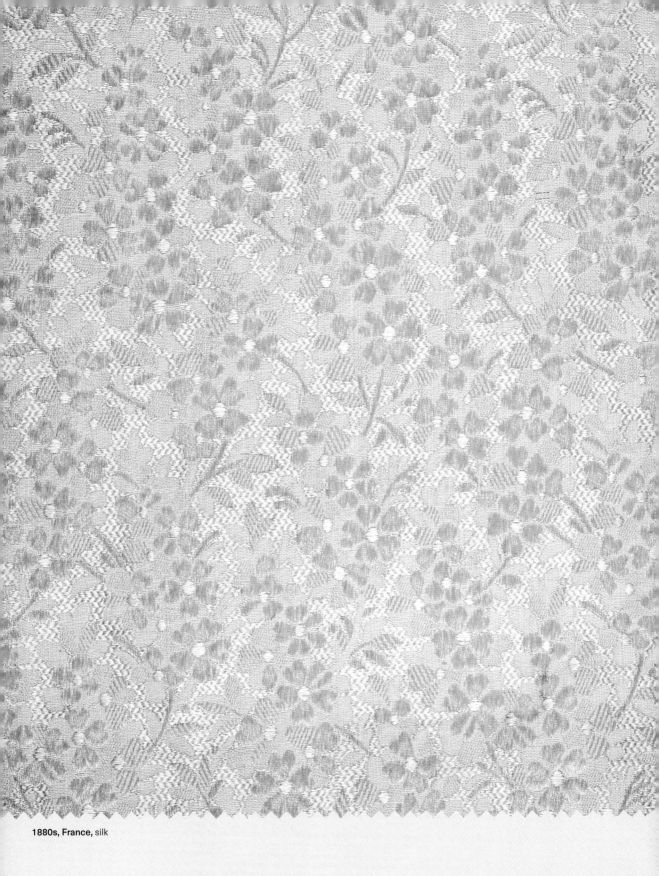

1880s, France, silk

1955, USA, synthetic

1910s, France, silk

1920s, France, silk

1890s, France, silk

1890s, France, silk

c. 1900, France, silk

1910s, France, silk

c. 1900, France, silk

c. 1900, France, silk

1850s, France, silk

1890s, France, silk

1890s, France, silk

1880s, France, silk

1870s, France, silk

1860s, France, silk

1880s, France, silk

1880s, France, silk and metallic yarns

1990s, France, silk

1880s, France, silk

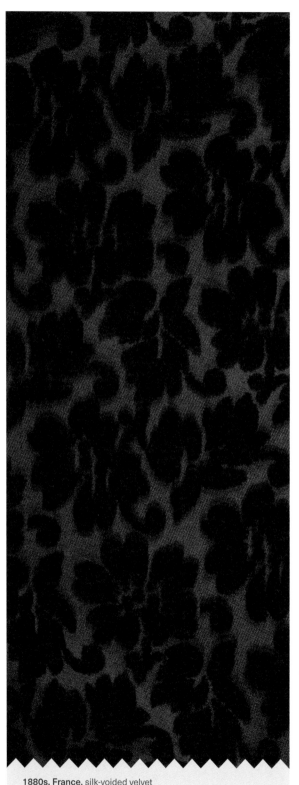

1880s, France, silk-voided velvet

1880s, France, silk-voided velvet

1880s, France, silk-voided velvet

1880s, France, silk-voided velvet

1870s, France, silk-voided velvet

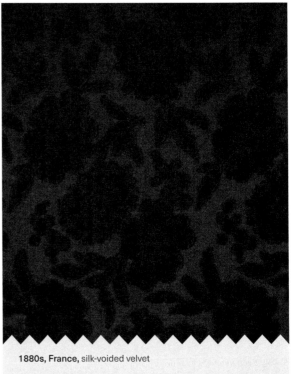

1880s, France, silk-voided velvet

1920s, France, silk-voided velvet

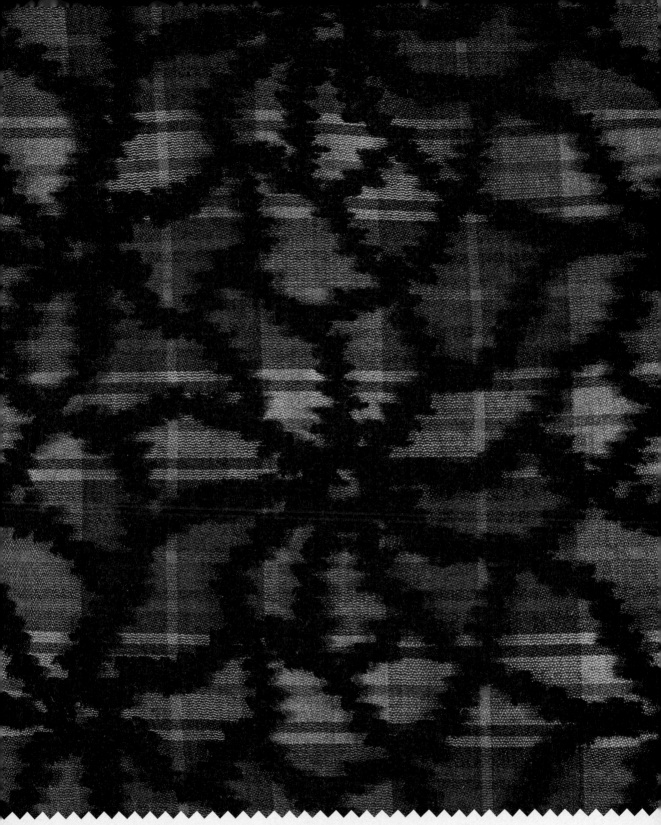

1890s, France, silk-voided velvet

Chapter 6
Paisley

Chapter 6

Paisley

The paisley motif, now referred to simply as "paisley," has its roots deep in the artwork of India. A derivation of a seed cone, paisley originally took textile form in intricately woven shawls developed in Kashmir, India, which were highly prized. Napoleon's troops brought these rare, expensive shawls home from their military campaigns at the turn of the nineteenth century, and the Empress Josephine, soon an avid collector, began the trend for wearing the delicately luxurious and sumptuously patterned goat-hair wraps.

As their popularity grew, the French, then the English set out to rival the Indian designs. Although they would never equal the meticulous weave of the Kashmir originals, Europeans had the advantage of the jacquard loom: a French device that made its debut in 1804 and could create elaborately woven fabrics in a much simpler way. The town of Paisley, Scotland, already known as a textile town, set out to become the foremost weavers of these shawls. Such was their success that this pattern now bears the town's name.

These shawls were highly fashionable through the early reign of Queen Victoria, but the fad eventually evaporated in the 1880s. Many later Victorian and early Edwardian garments were fashioned from the remaining shawl fabric that was found abandoned in attics.

A paisley revival in the 1950s initially manifested itself in small-scale conservative designs with muted colors, but by 1965 paisleys were all the rage. These later iterations are bright and exuberant, with the scale blown out of proportion (see pages 290–291). Wild and psychedelic, they enjoyed a great revival into the early 1970s. Though the popularity has waned again, paisley remains a popular print, much like your most comfortable worn-in tweed blazer.

1860s, Scotland,
machine-woven
wool

1860s, France, roller-printed wool

1860s, France, roller-printed wool

1860s, France, roller-printed wool

1860s, France, roller-printed wool

1860s, France, roller-printed cotton

1860s, France, roller-printed wool

1860s, France, roller-printed wool

c. 1883, France, silk brocade

1880s, France, silk brocade

1880s, France, silk brocade

1870s, Scotland, machine-woven wool

1870s, France, roller-printed wool with metallic embroidery

1870s, France or Scotland, machine-woven wool

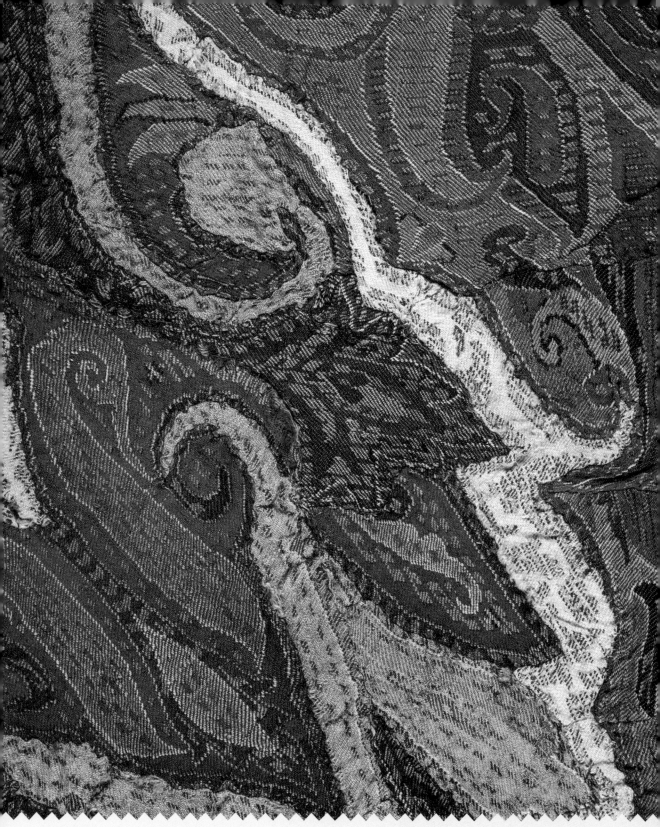

1870s, India, hand-woven and pieced wool

1820s, France, machine-woven wool

1820s, France, machine-woven wool

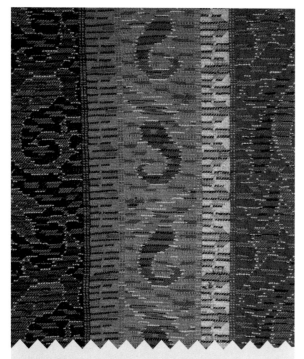

1850s, France or Scotland, machine-woven wool

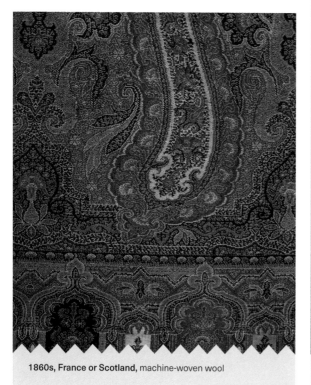

1860s, France or Scotland, machine-woven wool

1840s, India, hand-woven wool

1860s, Scotland, machine-woven wool

1860s, India, hand-woven and embroidered wool

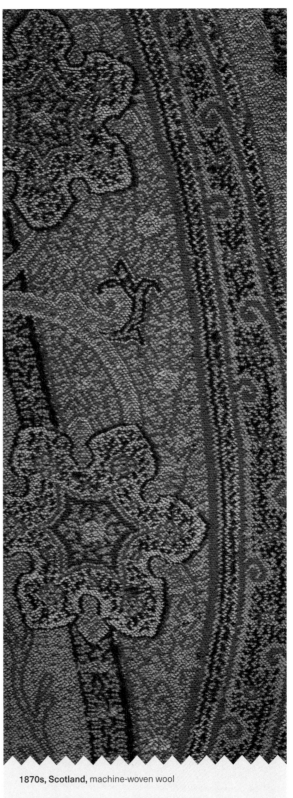

1870s, Scotland, machine-woven wool

1870s, Scotland, machine-woven wool

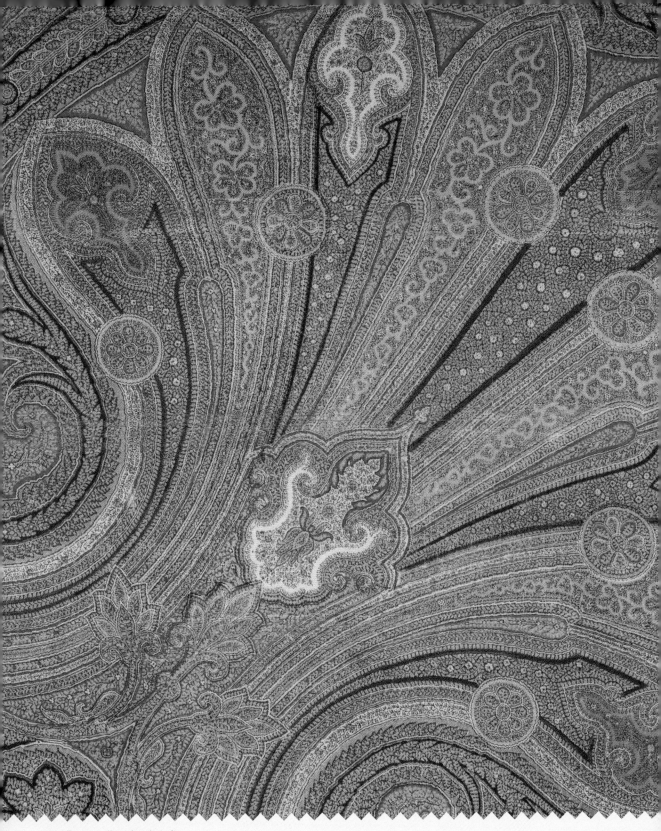

1860s, France, roller-printed wool

1860s, Scotland, machine-woven wool

1850s, France, machine-woven wool

1840s, India, hand-woven wool

1860s, India, hand-embroidered wool

1850s, France or Scotland, machine-woven wool

1860s, Scotland, machine-woven wool

1860s, France, roller-printed wool

1860s, France, roller-printed wool

1860s, France, roller-printed wool

c. 1865, France, roller-printed wool

1880s, USA, roller-printed cotton

1860s, France, roller-printed wool

c. 1967, USA, screen-printed cotton

c. 1967, USA, roller-printed synthetic

c. 1967, USA, roller-printed synthetic

c. 1967, USA, roller-printed synthetic

1970s, USA, roller-printed synthetic

1970s, USA, roller-printed synthetic

1970s, USA, roller-printed synthetic

1970s, USA, roller-printed synthetic

c. 1947, USA, roller-printed synthetic

1980s, USA, roller-printed synthetic

1980s, USA, roller-printed cotton

1980s, France, roller-printed silk

c. 1967, USA, roller-printed synthetic

1970s, USA, roller-printed cotton

c. 1967, USA, roller-printed synthetic

1940s, USA, roller-printed cotton

c. 1967, USA, roller-printed synthetic

c. 1967, USA, roller-printed synthetic

c. 1967, USA, roller-printed cotton

Credits

The following garments/textiles are courtesy of the Rochester Museum & Science Center (accession numbers provided). All other garments/textiles are from the Sue Ann Genet Costume Collection.

Floral
p. 14   MTH 9023
p. 17   MTH 33037
p. 18   UL: MTH 3481; UR: MTH 8920; LL: MTH 16029; LR: MTH 39098
p. 19   UL: MTH 39097; UR: MTH 46031; LR: 2019.00.50
p. 20   UL: 93.82.6; UR: MTH 31071; LL: MTH 33050; LR: NN
p. 26   UL: MTH 1168; UR: MTH 37099-64.82
p. 28   MTH 41082
p. 32   UL: MTH 34008, UR: MTH 12013, LR: 82.188.1
p. 33   UL: 80.207.8; UR: MTH 300; LL: MTH 4594
p. 38   LL: NN; LR: MTH 8373
p. 46   UR: MTH 10009; LL: MTH 46032
p. 50   UL: MTH 3897; UR: 72.66.6; LL: MTH 8559; LR: 38.77 MTH 2795
p. 51   left: MTH 65173; right: MTH 23095
p. 52   UR: 79.266.2; LL: MTH 5261
p. 56   LL: MTH 33083
p. 57   UL: MTH 3805
p. 58   MTH 5062
p. 59   left: MTH 654150
p. 60   LL: MTH 5980; right: NN
p. 61   UL: MTH 5873; LL: MTH 33056 61.326; right: MTH 7804
p. 63   MTH 7145
p. 64   left: MTH 316; UR: MTH 4829; LR: MTH 864
p. 65   left: MTH 7979; UR: MTH 65540, LR: MTH 9019-51.341
p. 66   76.178.2
p. 67   MTH 2202

Geometric
p. 78   UL: MTH 46027; UR: MTH 3370
p. 79   LL: MTH 16035; LR: MTH 1530-41.190
p. 80   LL: MTH 3401 38.176
p. 81   UL: NN
p. 82   MTH 65565
p. 92   MTH 37002
p. 94   MTH 40357
p. 95   upper: NN; LL: MTH 2791-42.10
p. 100 left: 84.146.3; right: MTH 4033
p. 102 MTH 5826
p. 103 right: MTH 42107
p. 104 UL: MTH 7555; UR: MTH 7555; LL: MTH 4072; LR: MTH 6329
p. 105 UL: MTH 2699–41.190; LL: MTH 300, LR: MTH 1696
p. 106 lower: 83.123.31
p. 107 right: MTH 18064
p. 108 MTH 41127
p. 109 MTH 5148
p. 110 left: NN; right: MTH 3873

Conversational
p. 116 left: MTH 28019; right: 65415-66.234
p. 117 upper: MTH 9223; lower: MTH 10.800
p. 118 upper: NN; lower: MTH 18080
p. 119 MTH 9667
p. 127 UL: MTH 3259
p. 130 MTH 2959
p. 131 MTH 16021
p. 132 left: MTH 7207
p. 135 90.5849
p. 140 lower: MTH 41124
p. 144 lower: MTH 6609
p. 145 MTH 42100
p. 147 UR: MTH 8846
p. 154 upper: MTH 8406; lower: NN
p. 157 left: MTH 7124
p. 158 left: NN; right: MTH 10118
p. 159 left: NN
p. 164 lower: MTH 7622
p. 178 left: MTH 8259; right: MTH 5609
p. 188 MTH 27002

Constructed Pattern
p. 194 MTH 16086
p. 196 UL: MTH 7795; LL: 79.395.1; right MTH 309
p. 197 MTH 3873
p. 198 UL: MTH 4792; UR: MTH 4792; lower: MTH 44030
p. 199 UL: MTH 4562; UR: MTH 4637; LR: MTH 65662 67.205.69
p. 200 MTH 7623
p. 201 UL: MTH 65662 67.205.69; UR: MTH 9570; LL: MTH 7623; LR: MTH 40182
p. 202 UL: MTH 4263; LL: MTH 6963
p. 203 MTH 9782
p. 204 left: MTH 27038; right: MTH 3001
p. 205 left: NN; right: NN
p. 206 left: MTH 27038; right: MTH 27038
p. 207 upper: MTH 9782; lower: MTH 9782

Acknowledgments

Dr. Michael S. Tick, Dean, College of Visual and Performing Arts, Syracuse University

Dr. James Fathers, Director, School of Design, VPA, SU

Kirsten Schoonmaker, Collections Manager, Sue Ann Genet Costume Collection, Assistant Teaching Professor SU

Sally Tomkins, Professor of Practice, Fashion Design, SU

Sarah Wilson LeCount, Collections Manager, Rochester Museum & Science Center

Elizabeth Pietrzykowski, Registrar, RMSC

Stephanie Ball, Archivist and Librarian, RMSC

Kathryn Murano-Santos, Senior Director for Collections and Exhibits, RMSC

Jeffrey Mayer would like to thank the following:
Carolyn and Ellsworth Mayer
Susan Mayer
Margaret Mayer
The memory of Martha Caldwell, Professor Emeritus of Clothing, Textiles and Design, University of Vermont

Todd Conover would like to thank the following:
Gary Jones
The memory of his mother Linda Runyon

Lauren Tagliaferro would like to thank the following:
Dr. Stephen Polly
David and Nancy Tagliaferro

Thank you to commissioning editor Sara Goldsmith for championing this project, to Katherine Pitt for her tireless editing, and to Eleanor Ridsdale for her beautiful design.

Special acknowledgments to the family of Sue and Leon Genet for their continued support of the Sue Ann Genet Costume Collection:
Pam Genet Barsh
Wendy Genet Kaplan
Jill Genet Waller